EVERYDAY
CURRIES

EVERYDAY
CURRIES

Carolyn Humphries

SPRING HILL

Published by Spring Hill, an imprint of How To Books Ltd
Spring Hill House, Spring Hill Road
Begbroke, Oxford OX5 1RX
United Kingdom
Tel: (01865) 375794
Fax: (01865) 379162
info@howtobooks.co.uk
www.howtobooks.co.uk

First published 2013

How To Books greatly reduce the carbon footprint of their books
by sourcing their typesetting and printing in the UK.

British Library Cataloguing in Publication Data
A catalogue record of this book is available from the British Library.

ISBN: 978 1 905862 92 4

Produced for How To Books by I̶ᴇ̶ʀ̶ ̶P̶a̶r̶k̶ ̶P̶r̶o̶d̶u̶c̶t̶i̶o̶n̶s̶,̶ ̶T̶a̶v̶i̶s̶t̶o̶c̶k̶,̶ ̶D̶e̶v̶o̶n̶
Designed and typeset by Mousen
Edited by Wendy Hobson
Printed and bound by in Great B

Contents

Introduction

If you're reading this book, then you already like curries. Whether you usually have a takeaway treat on Friday night, already cook the odd one or two at home, or enjoy eating in local restaurants, you'll know that those fragrant spices, delicious textures and heady aromas tickle your taste buds. Well, in this book I've put together some of my favourite curries from around the world and added some creations of my own to make a whole compendium from creamy mild ones to blow-the-roof-off-your-mouth fiery ones. Whatever your preference, there's something for you here.

For some of the Indian-style dishes, I have made spice pastes because grinding your own spices gives the best flavour and is very satisfying to do. However, not everyone has the time or inclination for that – and it does take a little time – so for most of the dishes I have used ground spice and pastes. They still taste great, I promise you, but there's less work for you.

You'll also find that there are loads of accompaniments to serve with your curries, from guidance on how to make the fluffiest basmati rice to breads, pickles and side dishes, plus some delicious spicy salads. Some are really quick and easy; others take a little more time. None is complicated.

While some curries are very quick to make, others benefit from a long, slow cooking time to tenderise the meat and really develop the flavours. But even those dishes that do need longer cooking are quick to prepare and can just to be left on their own to cook while you get on with something else, so the recipes still take up very little of your time. Plus, those of you who like pressure cooking or slow cooking – to speed things up or slow things down to suit your lifestyle – will find instructions on how to adapt the recipes to suit your chosen method.

Many people claim that their version of a particular recipe is the authentic one – a claim that is not easy to substantiate, either in the world of curries or any other style of cooking! I make no such promises. What I do promise is a collection of great-tasting recipes that you will enjoy and that will spur you on to experiment with your own combinations of ingredients.

Especially for those who are new to spicy food, or those who only enjoy mild curries, each recipe is marked with a rating, a tiny chilli ♪. They will give you an idea of where the recipe falls on the scale of 'spicy' on a scale of one to three. These heat ratings will give you a good indication of how much heat to expect, but do remember that everyone tolerates chilli differently so they can only serve as a guide. And, of course, you have infinite possibilities to reduce or increase the quantity of spices, and especially chillis, in any dish so that it suits your own palate. Never be afraid to reduce the quantity of spices – or increase it – in any recipe; if you like it, that's what counts.

So make a start and enjoy Everyday Curries. It will take you on your own spice-route journey, providing you with the wherewithal to make delicious curries to awaken imaginative and exciting taste sensations that will have you coming back for more!

CHAPTER 1 Storecupboard Standbys

If your cupboard is bare at the end of the week, then it stands to reason that you won't be able to put together a quick meal or respond if someone drops in and you want to offer them supper. On the other hand, if you always have a few basic items in the cupboard – cans of tomatoes and pulses, spices and herbs, flour, beans, rice and so on – you will always be able to throw together an interesting meal for yourself or for family and guests.

I've listed here a good selection of items you might like to keep in your storecupboard so that you can include a whole range of curries in your repertoire.

You'll notice that I've called for quite a lot of individual spices. That's because to make a reasonable selection of simple curries, as we do in this book, you need to have a good selection. Most of those I've used are likely to be familiar already, or soon will be once you begin to cook the recipes as you'll use them quite frequently. Occasionally, however, you may come across an ingredient you haven't used before. Just head for the spice section of your local supermarket, or ethnic store, and they will all be quite readily available. Plus, it's fun to experiment (particularly if you are a curry addict!) and you'll be learning all the time.

Spices start to deteriorate as soon as they're ground, which is why traditional curry cooks will always grind their own spices just before cooking. To help you achieve that authentic flavour, some of these recipes involve making your own spice paste. That's great fun and very rewarding but perhaps not something you will want to do every time, so you will always be given the option of using a ready-prepared spice mix instead, if you prefer. After all, this is an 'everyday' curry book, and if your lifestyle is anything like mine, you are unlikely to be grinding spices every day. I am assuming you just want to create great-tasting curries in the simplest way possible, so I have also included many recipes using ready-ground spices.

For a few simple recipes where I've called for a pre-prepared Indian spice mix, I have generally used a Madras curry paste or powder as that is a popular, medium-spiced paste that gives a great flavour. If you know you like your curries mild, you can simply replace the Madras with a mild Korma powder or paste, for example, or if you like it hot, go for something like a Vindaloo or another hot option. As I've said, never feel you cannot alter a recipe to suit your own taste.

The other ingredients listed on these pages offer you a guide to what you'd need if you wanted to cook the whole book, but I know you aren't going to go out and buy everything in one go! Try a couple of recipes. If you like them, then start stocking up on your storecupboard essentials by adding one or two extra items to your weekly shopping list until you have, gradually and imperceptibly, built up a stock of ingredients to allow you to create a sensational curry whenever the mood takes you!

Always keep your dried herbs and spices in small quantities in a dark, cool cupboard. That way they'll keep their colour and fragrance for several months. If you do tidy up the cupboard and find they have been lurking at the back for too long, throw them out as they will no longer have a good flavour.

Store opened jars and bottles of pureés and sauces in the fridge to keep them fresh as long as possible.

Keep fresh vegetables in the chiller box in the fridge (except roots and tubers, which are best in a rack in cool, dark cupboard).

Frozen chopped onions (and shallots too) are a boon for any busy cook. Keep a bag in the freezer and just take out handfuls of as you need them – so quick and no tears!

Bottles, jars and tubes
Chilli sauces: sweet and hot
Honey, clear
Jalapeño peppers, pickled
Lemon juice
Lime juice
Lime pickle
Mango chutney
Miso paste: red and/or white
Oils: olive, sunflower, sesame
Olives: stoned black and green (whole and/or sliced)
Passata
Soy sauces: dark and light
Stock concentrates or cubes: chicken, beef, vegetable
Thai fish sauce
Tomato purée
Vinegars: white/red wine, malt, rice
Worcestershire sauce

Cans
Baked beans
Butter beans
Chickpeas
Coconut milk
Lentils, green
Pinto beans
Sweetcorn
Tomatoes, chopped

Dry goods
Breads, vacuum-packed: chapattis, naan, pittas
Flour: plain, self-raising, wholemeal, gram, cornflour
Pearl barley

Coconut: desiccated, creamed
Dried fruit: sultanas, raisins, currants
Shiitake mushrooms, dried
Lentils, red
Noodles: Chinese medium egg, rice, udon
Popadoms, dried
Rice: basmati, jasmine
Sugars: caster, soft light brown
Tofu, firm

Dried Herbs, spices, nuts and seeds
Allspice
Asafoetida
Basil
Bay leaves (or fresh if you have them in your garden)
Cardamom pods
Chilli: powder and dried flakes
Chinese five-spice powder
Cinnamon, ground and sticks
Cloves, whole and ground
Coriander, ground and seeds
Cumin, ground and seeds
Curry leaves
Fennel and/or caraway seeds
Fenugreek, ground
Galangal purée
Garam masala
Garlic cloves or purée
Ginger, fresh root or purée
Kaffir lime leaves (use fresh instead if you prefer)
Lemongrass stalks or purée
Madras curry powder or paste
Mint
Mixed spice
Mustard powder
Nutmeg, preferably whole to grate but otherwise ground
Nuts: ground and flaked almonds, raw cashews, roasted (preferably unsalted) peanuts,
Onion and/or garlic granules
Oregano
Paprika, sweet

Pepper, freshly ground
Salt
Seeds: black mustard, black onion, caraway, fennel, sesame
Star anise
Tamarind paste
Tandoori powder or paste
Thai red and green curry paste
Turmeric, ground

Fridge
Butter and/or ghee
Milk, semi-skimmed
Cheese, feta
Cream: single, double, crème fraîche
Eggs
Paneer
Yoghurt, thick plain

Frozen foods
Chicken breasts, skinless
Herbs: coriander, parsley
Meat: lamb neck, pork fillets, minced lamb and beef
Onions/shallots, chopped
Root vegetables, mixed
Pastry: filo, shortcrust
Peas
Soya beans
Spinach

Everyday fresh vegetables and fruit
Carrots
Chillies
Cucumber
Herbs: basil and or horapa (Thai basil) coriander, mint, parsley
Lemons
Lettuce
Limes
Onions: brown, red, shallots, spring
Peppers
Potatoes
Tomatoes

Cooking for the Freezer

2

Many of the curries in this book are suitable for freezing and, since you are clearly a fan, it makes sense to cook in larger quantities than you need so that you can serve some straight away and save some for another day.

Each recipe indicates how long it can be kept in the freezer or, in a few instances, if it is unsuitable for freezing.

Sometimes a dish needs to be frozen without the final garnishing or finishing ingredients, in which case the extra instructions will be provided. If the final ingredients have been omitted for freezing, simply thaw and reheat the dish when required, then stir in the remaining ingredients before serving.

How to freeze
The method for freezing is simple.
- Complete the dish, taking into account any special freezing instructions.
- Leave the dish to cool completely; this should be done as quickly as possible.
- Spoon curries into a rigid freezer container and close the lid. Items such as bhajis can be placed in a freezer bag and sealed tightly.
- Label clearly with the name of the dish and the date.
- Put in the freezer for up to the recommended length of time.

Defrosting
Defrost in the fridge or at room temperature and make sure you reheat thoroughly. Don't reheat more than once.

CHAPTER 3

Planning Your Meal

Whether you're having friends round, celebrating a special family occasion or just having a Saturday night in, you might like to plan a complete spiced meal from the book. Here are some basic principles to help you put together a beautifully balanced meal, as that is what you need to think about in order to ensure that your dishes complement each other perfectly. I've also included a few sample menus to highlight individual styles, so you can see how the whole meal blends together beautifully, whatever style you're going for.

When you are planning a meal, there are various elements to consider to make sure it all works well together, including style, flavour, colour and texture. Let's have a look at each one in turn. Once you understand the principles, putting together beautifully balanced meals will be second nature.

Style
The first thing to think about is whether you want to focus on one individual international cuisine. That's a good thing to do if you are new to curry cooking, as the dishes will be designed to relate to each other, using similar spices and ingredients. Once you become more adventurous, you might like to try mixing and matching cuisines. You might be surprised to find that they work together well, although you need to give some thought to whether they will complement each other in all the ways that are important.

Variety
It sounds obvious to say that if you choose a beef dish for your main course, then it's a good idea to have something different – fish or vegetables, perhaps – as the main ingredient for your starter. In most instances it's best to go for a balance of meat, fish and vegetables through the meal, so you would probably be best not to choose to

have chicken tikka, say, followed by tandoori chicken as it would be better to have something other than chicken for one of the courses.

Having said that, if you absolutely love fish, for example – as I do – there's enough variety to allow you to create a varied menu by having, say, a prawn starter with a sauce followed by a grilled or roast fish dish.

Flavour

Once you have selected your main ingredient to give you variety, you need to apply that principle through the other ingredients too. You wouldn't want everything to be tomato-based, for instance, or everything would have a similar underlying flavour. You need a good mix. As well as repeating chicken, chicken tikka and tandoori chicken are also both yoghurt-based, making them rather too similar to serve together. A better choice might be a grilled or fried starter made with beef or vegetables, for example.

Heat

How hot should you make your curry? Firstly, consider your guests – do they all like hot spices? If you know they like spicy dishes, then you have more scope, but if you have guests who prefer more subtle flavours – or if you don't know what they like – then keep things lower down the spicy scale.

Even if you know you are serving to hot-curry lovers, you still need a mix of recipes – some to fire you up, some to cool you down. Don't choose the triple chilli treatment for every dish. Mild, delicate flavours will complement the fire, not detract from it. If you have a selection, you will provide something for everyone.

Colour and presentation

Think of how much difference it makes to your appreciation of your meal that it looks fabulous as well as tasting great. So you need to consider each dish you are planning to cook and what it will look like alongside others that you are going to serve before it, after it or with it. It would look pretty unappetising to be served a meal of potato, chicken and cauliflower – not the most colourful combination! So make sure the ingredients are different colours. You don't want everything to be white, brown, red, yellow or green – you want a good mixture so each plate is appealing to the eye.

If you do find that, having got almost to serving-out time, you think your meal is not going to be as attractive as it might be, think about how to present it. You may be able to add a dash of colour with a few frozen peas, a garnish of some bright green fresh parsley or coriander or a lovely wedge of lemon.

Texture

Texture is vital in your planning, too. Mix smooth and soft with chunky and crunchy. A plateful of soft pap is for babies only – adults need a few elements to get their teeth into as well!

Putting it all together

Although this sounds like a lot to think about, it is very much common sense. If you work through the elements of your menu, thinking about one point at a time, it will soon become clear whether your choice is going to wow your guests – or not!

Suggested menus

At the end of a busy day – and on many other occasions, too, I expect – you will simply make one main meal for your supper or dinner dish. However, on some occasions you are likely to want to create a complete meal of several courses, so here are some suggested menus for various eating styles. You may want to cook these meals as a start, then go on to develop your own menus as you gain in confidence.

So here are a few ideas for delicious, balanced meals using the different styles of curry you'll find in this book. Remember, there are loads of fusion dishes that all blend beautifully together, too, for when you don't fancy a straight Indian or Thai meal, for instance. Experiment, find your favourites, then put them together using the balance guide above.

To help you in your planning, we have included a guide to the origins of each recipe, so you can see whether the original recipe originated in India, Asia, or other places around the world.

Indian-style supper

- Popadoms (page 134) with dips
- Prawn Pakoras with Fresh Tomato and Chilli Sauce (page 30)
- Goan-style Pork Curry (page 99) served with Plain Basmati Rice (page 128) and Carrot and Beetroot Salad with Mustard Yoghurt Dressing (page 140)
- Sweet Mango Lassi (page 146)
- Chai Ice-cream (page 150)

We often start an Indian meal with a few crisp popadoms to dip into a selection of pickles. You might want to add some chopped mint to plain yoghurt and serve that with your popadoms and some bought or home-made mango chutney and lime pickle, or perhaps some very finely shredded onion. This is usually followed by a more substantial starter, and for this menu I have chosen a fried prawn dish to complement the pork dish to follow.

The main course offers a colour and flavour contrast and is accompanied by plain rice and an interesting salad with a lively Indian influence. Finally, for dessert, a simple ice-cream, plus a smooth mango lasai to cool the fiery curry.

Far Eastern-style supper

- Beef Satay Sticks (page 34)
- Red Duck and Roasted Red Pepper Curry (page 66), Jasmine Rice (page 129), Stir-Fried Mangetout with Sweet Pepper (page 125)
- Mango Fool (page 152)

As I have chosen a lovely hot curry for the main course, I have teamed it with a beef starter to offer a contrast of flavours and textures, and concluded with a light and refreshing mango dessert, perfect for a hot Asian evening.

Caribbean-style supper

- Curried Corn and Sweet Potato Chowder (page 25)
- Caribbean Curried Lamb (page 92) with Simple Yellow Yellow Rice (page 7) and Avocado Sambal (page 144)
- Caramelised Pineapple and Banana with Buttered Rum (page 153)

Lively and colourful, as anything associated with the sunny Caribbean should be, this has all the hallmarks of those exotic islands with a spicy chowder to precede a lovely lamb curry, then a fruity, rum-laced pineapple dessert to provide a kick to finish.

Fusion-style supper

- Curried Cream of Carrot Soup (page 24)
- Curried Slow Roast Pork Belly with Crushed Potatoes and Spiced Green Salad (page 142)
- Chilli Chocolate Fondant (page 151)

If the flavours work well together, it really doesn't matter where they came from in the first place. Here's an adventurous menu with an international slant: a substantial, lightly spiced vegetable soup teamed with a modern, spiced-up version of the old-fashioned meat and two veg, and finished with an Inca-inspired chocolate dish with a dash of chilli.

CHAPTER 4

Notes and Conversion charts

For beginners, or for others who would like to familiarise themselves with the details of how the book is set out, here are a few notes on how the recipes are presented.

- Always preheat the oven and cook on the shelf just above the centre unless otherwise stated (this isn't necessary if you have a fan oven where the heat is similar throughout the oven).
- Always preheat the grill and cook food about 5cm from the heat source unless otherwise stated.
- The ingredients are listed in the order in which they are used in the recipe.
- All spoon measures are level unless otherwise stated.
- Eggs and vegetables are medium unless otherwise stated.
- Always wash, peel, core and deseed, if necessary, fresh produce before use. But deseeding fresh chillies is up to you (some say it reduces the heat to remove the seeds and white pith. If you like heat, leave them in!).
- Seasoning is very much a matter of personal taste. Taste the food as you cook and adjust to suit your own palate.
- Fresh herbs are great for adding flavour and colour. Pots of basil and parsley for your windowsill are particularly good (they keep best if left in the plastic wrapper). The others are best bought in bunches and kept in the chiller box in the fridge.
- All can and packet sizes are approximate as they vary from brand to brand.
- Cooking times are approximate and should be used as a guide. Always check food is piping hot and cooked through before serving.
- Information on freezing will be found on page 13. Recipes are indicated if they are suitable for freezing, with additional freezing information if relevant, or advised if not suitable.
- Each recipe is also marked with one, two or three chillis to give you can indication of how hot the dish is if you make it according

to the recipe given. Of course, you can adjust any recipe to suit your own taste.

♪♪♪ Very hot

♪♪ Moderately hot

♪ Mild

Recipes are also marked with a note of their origin.

African

Asian

British

Caribbean

Fusion

Indian

Conversion charts

Those who prefer imperial measures can use these conversions (they are approximate for ease of use).

For convenience, I sometimes use cup measures as it's so easy for things like rice or couscous. You can use American cup measuring sets, just an ordinary cup or a measuring jug. A cup is 250ml, or whatever volume fits into the space (so a cup of sugar is 225g whereas a cup of flour is 100g).

OVEN TEMPERATURES										
110°C	120°C	140°C	150°C	160°C	180°C	190°C	200°C	220°C	230°C	240°C
225°F	250°F	275°F	300°F	325°F	350°F	375°F	400°F	425°F	450°F	475°F
Gas ¼	Gas ½	Gas 1	Gas 2	Gas 3	Gas 4	Gas 5	Gas 6	Gas 7	Gas 8	Gas 9

WEIGHT										
25g	50g	75g	100g	150g	175g	200g	225g	250g	300g	450g
1oz	2oz	3oz	4oz	5oz	6oz	7oz	8oz	9oz	10oz	1lb

MEASUREMENTS										
5cm	10cm	13cm	15cm	18cm	20cm	25cm	30cm	35cm	40cm	45cm
2 in	4 in	5 in	6 in	7 in	8 in	10 in	12 in	14 in	16 in	18 in

LIQUID MEASURE										
5ml	15ml	50ml	75ml	100ml	125ml	150ml	200ml	300ml	450ml	600ml
1 tsp	1 tbsp	2 fl oz	3 fl oz	4 fl oz	4½ fl oz	5 fl oz	7 fl oz	½pt	¾pt	1pt

Soups and Starters

Curried soups are warming, soothing and sumptuous. They make perfect light meals for lunch or supper, served with some good bread and perhaps a light salad afterwards, or they can make the ideal starter if you adjust the quantities.

It's amazing how adding just a hint of spice to a vegetable soup can transform it into a dish with huge depths of flavour when, without it, the result could be fairly bland and uninteresting. The sweet root vegetables work particularly well for curried soups, as you'll discover.

I've also included my versions of some of the usual favourites: the bhajis, pakoras and samosas, the spicy kebabs and, just because I love them, a few small curried fusion dishes that would set the juices flowing for any dinner party.

Preparation time:
15 minutes
Cooking time:
2 hours
Freezeable for:
2 months

Serves 4 • British • ♪

Mulligatawny

Ingredients:
2 tbsp sunflower oil
1 onion, chopped
1 garlic clove, crushed
2 tbsp Madras curry powder
    or paste
1 meaty roast leg or
    shoulder lamb bone
About 1.5 litres boiling water
1 large carrot, diced
1 large potato, diced
¼ small cauliflower, cut in
    tiny florets
100g green beans, cut in
    short lengths (or use
    frozen)
1 green pepper, diced
1 fat green chilli, deseeded,
    if liked, and sliced
2 tbsp sultanas
1 tbsp tomato purée
50g red lentils
Salt and freshly ground black
    pepper
50g creamed coconut
A pinch of caster sugar
2 tbsp chopped fresh
    coriander

This traditional British/Indian soup is a great way to make a delicious and very substantial dish with the leftover lamb bone from the Sunday roast, or just use 3 pieces of scrag end of neck of lamb instead.

- Heat the oil in a large pan and fry the onion and garlic gently for 2 minutes, stirring.

- Stir in the curry powder or paste and fry for 30 seconds. Add the lamb bone, breaking it at the joints so it fits in the pan, and just cover with boiling water. Cover with a lid and bring to the boil, then reduce the heat and simmer gently for 1½ hours.

- Lift out the lamb and take all the meat off the bones. Cut the meat into small pieces and return the meat to the soup.

- Add the vegetables, chilli, sultanas, tomato purée, lentils and a little salt and pepper. Return to the boil, reduce the heat, cover and simmer gently for 30 minutes until everything is really tender.

- Stir in the creamed coconut until melted. Taste and add a pinch of sugar and more salt and pepper if required. Ladle into warm open soup bowls and serve sprinkled with the chopped coriander.

To slow cook: Prepare as above but put all the ingredients except the coconut, sugar and coriander in the slow cooker with 1.2 litres boiling water and cook on Low for 8–10 hours.

To pressure cook: Prepare as above using 1.2 litres boiling water and cook at High Pressure for 30 minutes. Remove the meat from the bone, return the meat to the cooker with the remaining ingredients except the coconut, sugar and coriander and cook at High Pressure for 5 minutes. Reduce the pressure quickly under cold water, stir in the coconut and sugar and season to taste.

Asian Chicken Noodle Soup with Eggs

This is based on a breakfast dish but I've given it a touch of elegance by using quails' eggs instead of wedges of hard-boiled hen's eggs, which turns it into a delicious light lunch dish or a starter for a couple more people.

- Cook the noodles according to the packet directions. Drain and set aside.

- Meanwhile, put the quails' eggs in a small pan of cold water. Bring to the boil and boil for 3 minutes. Drain and place immediately in cold water. Lightly roll each one on the work surface and remove the shells.

- Put everything except the eggs, chicken, coriander and crushed chilli flakes in a saucepan. Heat gently until it boils, which allows the flavours to develop, then reduce the heat and simmer for 3 minutes.

- Add the chicken, cover and simmer very gently for 5 minutes until the chicken is tender. Discard the lime leaves.

- Divide the noodles between warm open soup bowls. Ladle in the soup, making sure each person gets a fair amount of the chicken. Halve the eggs and divide amongst the bowls. Sprinkle with coriander and chilli flakes and serve.

Prepar
10
Not suita

Ingredients:
180g rice udon noodles
12 quails' eggs
4 spring onions, cut in short, diagonal slices
1 large garlic clove, crushed (or 1 tsp garlic purée)
1 tsp grated galangal or fresh root ginger (or galangal or ginger purée)
2 tsp finely chopped lemongrass (or lemongrass purée)
2 thin green chillies, deseeded, if liked, and finely chopped
1 tsp ground turmeric
1 tbsp Thai fish sauce
400ml can coconut milk
500ml chicken stock
2 kaffir lime leaves
2 skinless chicken breasts, cut in thin strips
2 tbsp chopped fresh coriander
1 tsp crushed dried chillies

ion time:
nutes
ooking time:
36 minutes
Freezeable for:
6 months without the milk or
cream

Serves 4–6 • British • 🌙

Curried Cream of Carrot Soup

Ingredients:
1 tbsp sunflower oil
1 onion, roughly chopped
2 tsp ground cumin
1 tsp ground turmeric
½ tsp ground coriander
¼ tsp chilli powder
4 large carrots, sliced
1 potato, peeled and diced
900ml vegetable stock
1 bay leaf
Salt and freshly ground black
    pepper
150ml milk
5 tbsp double cream
1 tbsp chopped fresh
    coriander or mint

Warming, smooth and satisfying, you can ring the changes by adding two parsnips or half a celeriac instead of two of the carrots, if you wish, giving you options to create several different but equally delicious results.

- Heat the oil in a large saucepan. Add the onion and fry gently, stirring, for 3 minutes until softened but not browned.

- Add all the spices and fry for 30 seconds.

- Stir in the carrots and potato and fry, stirring, for 2 minutes.

- Add the stock, bay leaf and some salt and pepper. Bring to the boil, reduce the heat, part-cover and simmer gently for 30 minutes until the vegetables are really soft.

- Discard the bay leaf and purée the soup in a blender or food processor.

- Return the soup to the saucepan, stir in the milk and cream, taste and re-season. Reheat but do not boil.

- Ladle into soup bowls, garnish with the chopped coriander or mint and serve hot.

To slow cook: Prepare as above but use only 700ml stock. Bring to the boil, tip into the slow cooker and cook on Low for 6–8 hours. Add the milk and cream re-cover and cook for a further few minutes until hot through.

To pressure cook: Prepare as above but use only 700ml stock. Pressure cook at High Pressure for 10 minutes, then reduce the pressure quickly under cold water and finish as before.

• Soups and Starters

Serves 4–6 • Fusion • 🌶

Curried Corn and Sweet Potato Chowder

Preparation time:
10 minutes
Cooking time:
25 minutes
(including making the stock)
Freezeable for:
6 months

I've given you the method using fresh corn cobs for this tasty chowder recipe but you can use 200g frozen sweetcorn (or a small can) instead when corn is not in season or if you are short of time and continue from step 3.

- Remove the silks and husks from the corn. Hold the cob firmly upright on a plate and cut off the kernels in a downward slice all round. Repeat with the other cob and set the kernels aside.

- Put the cobs in a saucepan and cover with the stock. Bring to the boil and boil for 5 minutes to extract the flavour. Strain the stock into a bowl and discard the cobs.

- In the same saucepan, melt the butter and fry the onion gently, stirring, for 3 minutes until softened and lightly golden.

- Add the curry powder and cinnamon and fry, stirring, for 30 seconds. Stir in the reserved stock, the sweet potato, potato, carrot and corn kernels. Bring back to the boil, then reduce the heat, part-cover and simmer gently for 15 minutes until the vegetables are soft.

- Ladle about half the vegetables into a blender with a little of the stock. Blend until smooth.

- Return the soup to the pan and season to taste with salt and pepper. Stir in most of the chopped coriander.

- Ladle into bowls, add a dollop of crème fraîche to each one and sprinkle the last of the coriander on top.

Ingredients:
2 corn cobs
1.2 litres vegetable stock
Large knob of butter
1 onion, finely chopped (or 1 large handful of frozen diced onion)
1 tbsp Madras curry powder or paste
1 tsp ground cinnamon
1 small sweet potato, peeled and finely diced
1 potato, peeled and finely diced
1 carrot, finely diced
120ml milk
Salt and freshly ground black pepper
4–6 tbsp crème fraîche
2 tbsp chopped fresh or frozen coriander

Preparation time:
10 minutes
Cooking time:
6 minutes
Freezeable for:
3 months

Makes 12 • Indian • ♪

Cauliflower Bhajis

Ingredients:
75g gram (chickpea) or plain
  flour
1 tsp ground cumin
1 tsp ground turmeric
½ tsp ground coriander
½ tsp chilli powder
¼ tsp salt
Good pinch of caster sugar
2 tbsp chopped fresh or
  frozen coriander
120ml plain yoghurt
2 tbsp milk
¼ cauliflower, white only,
  stump removed
Sunflower oil, for frying

To serve
Mango chutney

These delicious bites make a wonderful starter or you can serve them as an appetiser with drinks. There are many delicious chutneys and pickles in the shops, but why not try making your own Fresh Mango Chutney from the recipe on page 138.

- Mix together the flour, spices, salt, sugar and coriander. Stir in the yoghurt and milk to form a thick, creamy batter.

- Cut the cauliflower into slices about 5mm thick, then chop them into 1cm pieces. Stir into the batter.

- Heat about 1cm oil in a large frying pan until the tip of a teaspoonful of the batter, when dropped into the oil, sizzles furiously and rises to the surface immediately.

- Add 6 spoonfuls of the cauliflower batter mixture to the hot oil around the edges of the pan and fry for about 3 minutes, turning once, until golden and cooked through.

- Remove with a slotted spoon and drain on kitchen paper. Keep them warm whilst cooking and draining the remainder.

- Serve hot or warm with mango chutney.

Onion Bhajis

Preparation time:
10 minutes
Cooking time:
6 minutes
Freezeable for:
3 months

This has to be almost everyone's favourite Indian starter and while there are always lots of variations, the common factor of the succulent onions encased in that lightly spiced batter is what makes us all come back for more.

- Mix together the flour, spices, salt, sugar and coriander. Stir in the yoghurt and milk to form a thick, creamy batter.

- Stir the onions into the batter so they are well incorporated.

- Heat about 1cm oil in a large frying pan until the tip of a teaspoonful of the batter, when dropped into the oil, sizzles furiously and rises to the surface immediately.

- Add 6 spoonfuls of the onion batter mixture to the hot oil around the edges of the pan and fry for about 3 minutes, turning once, until golden and cooked through.

- Remove with a slotted spoon and drain on kitchen paper. Keep warm whilst cooking the remainder.

- Serve with a selection of pickles and an onion and tomato salad.

Ingredients:
75g gram (chickpea) or plain flour
1 tsp ground cumin
1 tsp ground turmeric
½ tsp ground coriander
½ tsp chilli powder
¼ tsp salt
Good pinch of caster sugar
2 tbsp chopped fresh or frozen coriander
120ml plain yoghurt
2 tbsp milk
2 large onions, chopped
Sunflower oil, for frying

To serve
Mango chutney
Lime pickle
Onion and tomato salad

Preparation time:
40 minutes
Cooking time:
6–8 minutes
Freezeable for:
3 months

Makes 16 • Indian • ♪

Meat Samosas

Ingredients:

For the dough
150g plain flour
A pinch of salt
1 tbsp sunflower oil
100ml cold water

For the filling
125g lean minced lamb or
    beef
1 small potato, peeled and
    finely diced
2 spring onions, chopped
¼ tsp chilli powder
1 tsp garam masala
A small handful of frozen
    peas
2 tsp tomato purée
2 tsp mango chutney
Salt and freshly ground black
    pepper

To finish
A little beaten egg
Oil, for frying

For this recipe, I've given the full instructions to make your own dough. It's not difficult and it is very satisfying. If you don't have the time or perhaps the inclination, follow the method using filo pastry from the Vegetable Samosas recipe on page 29.

- First, make the dough. Put the flour and salt in a bowl. Add the oil and mix in enough of the cold water to form a soft but not sticky dough. Wrap in clingfilm and leave to rest whilst making the filling.

- Put the meat, potato and spring onions in a small saucepan. Heat gently, stirring until the juices start to run, then raise the heat and fry a little more quickly, stirring until the grains of meat are separate and no longer pink.

- Stir in the chilli and garam masala, turn down the heat again, cover and cook very gently until the potato is tender and the juices have been absorbed, about 5 minutes. Stir in the remaining filling ingredients and season to taste. Set aside to cool.

- Divide the dough into 8 small balls. Roll each one out on a lightly floured surface to a circle about 12cm in diameter. Cut each one in half. Brush the cut edges with beaten egg. Fold each semi-circle into a cone shape. Hold in your hand and add a heaped teaspoonful of the filling. Press in well, then press the top rounded edges inside with a little beaten egg and press together to seal. Repeat with the remaining semi-circles and filling.

- Heat about 1cm sunflower oil in a frying pan until a cube of day-old bread browns in 30 seconds. Fry the samosas in two batches for 3–4 minutes until crisp and golden, turning once or twice.

• Soups and Starters

Makes 16 • Indian • 🌶

Vegetable Samosas

Preparation time:
30 minutes
Cooking time:
6–12 or 15–20 minutes
(depending on cooking
method)
Freezeable for:
3 months

These are made these using filo pastry for speed but you can use the dough for the meat samosas on page 28 if you prefer. They can be baked or fried and you can make large ones by cutting fewer, larger circles if you prefer.

- Peel the potato, cut in small pieces and boil until tender, then drain and mash. Or prick it all over, microwave for about 4 minutes until soft and then, when cool enough, peel and mash.

- Heat 1 tbsp oil in a frying pan and fry the onion for 3 minutes, stirring until soft and lightly golden.

- Add the spices and fry for 30 seconds. Remove from the heat and tip into the potato. Add the peas and enough of the reserved liquid from the can to moisten the mixture thoroughly so it is soft but not wet (you may need nearly all of it depending on the potato). Stir in the coriander. Mix thoroughly and set aside to cool.

- Preheat the oven to 200°C/Gas 6 (if baking).

- Brush a sheet of filo with a little oil. Top with a second sheet. Cut out 4 circles, about 12cm in diameter. Cut each one in half to form semi-circles. Repeat with the remaining two sheets of filo. Brush the cut edges with beaten egg. Fold each semi-circle into a cone shape. Hold in your hand and add a heaped teaspoonful of the filling. Press in well, then press the top rounded edges inside with a little beaten egg and press together to seal. Repeat with the remaining semi-circles and filling.

- Bake in the oven for 15–20 minutes until crisp and golden. Alternatively, heat about 1cm sunflower oil in a large frying pan until a cube of day-old bread browns in 30 seconds and fry the samosas in a few batches for 3–4 minutes, turning once or twice.

- Serve hot or cold with mango chutney or carrot raita.

Ingredients:
1 large potato (about 225g)
1 tbsp sunflower oil, plus
    extra for brushing (and
    frying, if necessary)
1 small onion, chopped (or a
    handful of frozen chopped
    onion)
1 tsp ground cumin
¼ tsp chilli powder
1 tsp ground turmeric
1 tsp garam masala
300g can of garden peas in
    water, drained, reserving
    the water
1 tbsp chopped fresh or
    frozen coriander
Salt and freshly ground black
    pepper
4 sheets of filo pastry

To serve
Fresh Mango Chutney (page
    138) or use bought
Carrot Raita (page 136)

Preparation time:
10 minutes
Cooking time:
4–6 minutes
Freezeable for:
6 months for the sauce,
2 months for the pakoras

Prawn Pakoras with Fresh Tomato and Chilli Sauce

Ingredients:

For the sauce
2 fairly large ripe tomatoes, skinned
½ tsp chilli powder
1 tsp clear honey
1 tsp lime juice
1 tbsp tomato purée
Pinch of salt

For the pakoras
75g gram (chickpea) or wholemeal flour
1 tsp ground cumin
6 tbsp water
2 spring onions, finely chopped
1 fat green chilli, deseeded, if liked, and finely chopped
300g cooked, peeled cold water prawns, thawed and dried if frozen
¼ tsp bicarbonate of soda
Sunflower oil, for frying

These delicious little bite-sized morsels taste good with finely diced paneer (Indian cheese) instead of prawns if you are looking for a vegetarian option. Paneer is readily available from major supermarkets or ethnic stores.

- To make the sauce, purée the tomatoes in a blender with the remaining sauce ingredients, seasoning to taste with salt. Transfer to a small dish and chill until ready to serve.

- To make the pakoras, mix the flour with the cumin, ½ tsp salt and the water to form a thick batter. Stir in the remaining ingredients except the frying oil.

- Heat about 1cm of oil in a large frying pan until a tip of a teaspoonful of the batter dropped into it sizzles furiously and rises to the surface. Using about half the batter, drop teaspoonfuls of the mixture into the oil and fry for 2–3 minutes until golden. Remove with a slotted spoon and drain on kitchen paper. Keep warm whilst cooking the remainder.

- Pile on a plate and serve hot with the sauce.

Kofta Kebabs

Preparation time:
20 minutes
Cooking time:
10–12 minutes
Freezeable for:
3 months, but best served fresh

Similar whether Indian or Middle Eastern, I've made these slightly more Indian flavoured and served them with Indian accompaniments. Reduce the chilli for a milder kebab. They are delicious starter or a main course with rice or naans and salad.

- Preheat the grill and soak 8 wooden skewers.
- Mix all the kebab ingredients together with your hands, squeezing the mixture well to mix thoroughly.
- Divide into 8 equal pieces and shape each into a cylinder around the skewers, so they're about half the length of the sticks.
- Brush with oil and place on the grill rack. Grill for 10–12 minutes, turning once, until golden and cooked through.
- Serve with cucumber raita, popadoms and mango chutney.

Ingredients:

For the kebabs
600g lean minced lamb
2 large garlic cloves, crushed
   (or 2 tsp garlic purée)
1 small onion, grated
2 tsp ground cumin
1 tsp ground coriander
½ tsp chilli powder
1 tsp dried mint
2 tbsp chopped fresh or
   frozen coriander
Salt and freshly ground black
   pepper
1 egg, beaten
8 soaked wooden skewers
2 tbsp olive oil

To serve
Cucumber Raita (page 137)
Popadoms (page 134)
Fresh Mango Chutney (page
   138)

Preparation time:
20 minutes

Cooking time:
8–10 minutes

Freezeable for:
3 months

Makes 24 • Indian • ♪

Shami Kebabs

Ingredients:
400g can of chickpeas,
    drained
1 onion, roughly chopped
    (or a large handful of
    frozen, chopped onion)
2 garlic cloves, halved (or
    1 tsp garlic purée)
1 tsp grated fresh root
    ginger (or ginger purée)
1 tbsp Tandoori powder or
    paste
1 tsp garam masala
½ tsp ground cinnamon
¼ tsp ground cloves
Handful of fresh coriander
    leaves
Handful of fresh mint leaves
Salt and freshly ground black
    pepper
500g lean minced lamb
1 egg, beaten
A little sunflower oil
Lemon wedges, to garnish

To serve
Cucumber Raita (page 137)
    or Carrot Raita (page 136)
Fresh Mango Chutney (page
    138) or use bought

You need a food processor for these kebabs, which observe the tradition of using chickpeas with lamb. Some people use green or red lentils or split peas instead but they don't give the same texture and flavour. Use Madras curry paste instead of tandoori mix if you like.

- Crush the chickpeas, onion and garlic in a food processor, stopping and scraping down the sides until almost puréed.

- Add the spices, herbs and plenty of salt and pepper and run the machine again, stopping and scraping down the sides as necessary. Add the meat and pulses to mix together. Add the beaten egg and pulse again to bind.

- Preheat the grill, and line grill pan with oiled foil.

- Shape the mixture into 24 small patties, about 5cm in diameter, squeezing them together well with your hands. Brush all over with oil, grill for 4–5 minutes each side until golden and cooked through. Alternatively, you can fry them in a little oil in a hot pan.

- Pile onto a plate, garnish with lemon wedges and serve with raita and mango chutney to dip.

Chicken Tikka

Prepara_   _
10 minutes plus m_
Cooki_
15 minutes
Not suitable for freezing

Tikka means 'bits' and this is simply marinated chicken 'bits' grilled on skewers. Make sure you have the grill good and hot – or use a griddle to get nice charred bits as you cook them. They make a delicious starter or a main course with dal, rice and salad.

- Mix everything except the chicken in a large plastic container with a lid. Add the chicken, mix well, cover and leave in the fridge for at least 2 hours or all day or overnight, if more convenient.

- Preheat the grill and soak 8 wooden skewers for at least 30 minutes.

- Drain the chicken of excess marinade. Thread on the soaked wooden skewers. Grill, turning once or twice, for about 15 minutes or until cooked through and slightly charred at the edges.

- Serve hot with chapattis, lime pickle and mango chutney.

Ingredients:
90ml thick plain yoghurt
2 large garlic cloves (or 2 tsp garlic purée)
2 tsp grated fresh root ginger (or ginger purée)
½ tsp chilli powder
1 tbsp lemon or lime juice
1 tbsp sweet paprika
1 tbsp garam masala
1 tsp soft light brown sugar
¼ tsp salt
Freshly ground black pepper
2 tbsp finely chopped fresh or frozen coriander
500g skinless chicken breast, diced (or 4 small breasts, cut in bite-sized chunks)

To serve
Chapattis (page 133)
Lime pickle
Mango chutney

Preparation time:
15 minutes plus marinating
Cooking time:
4 minutes
Freezeable for:
3 months in the marinade before threading, but best eaten fresh

Ingredients:
450g beef frying steak

For the marinade
2 tbsp sunflower oil
1 tbsp lime juice
1 tsp finely chopped lemongrass (or lemongrass purée)
1 garlic clove, crushed (or ½ tsp garlic purée)
1 tsp grated fresh root ginger (or ginger purée)
2 tbsp light soy sauce
1 tsp sweet paprika
½ tsp chilli powder
12 wooden skewers, soaked

For the peanut sauce
175ml water
2 spring onions, finely chopped
8 tbsp crunchy peanut butter
1 tbsp clear honey
2 tbsp light soy sauce
2 tsp crushed dried chillies

Makes 12 • Asian • ♪♪

Beef Satay Sticks

I have done a chicken version of this before, but beef ones are excellent. Make sure you beat the meat very thin to tenderise it and marinate for at least two hours. The lime juice helps the process. You can thread each piece on a separate skewer if you prefer.

- Put the steaks in a plastic bag and beat with a meat mallet or rolling pin until thin and well flattened. Cut across the grain into 24 strips, about 2cm wide.

- Mix all the marinade ingredients together in a large, shallow sealable container. Add the beef slices and toss gently with your hands so they are all coated. Cover and place in the fridge to marinate for several hours or all day or overnight.

- Preheat the grill and soak 12 wooden skewers for at least 30 minutes.

- When nearly ready to serve, make the sauce. Put all the sauce ingredients in small saucepan and heat, stirring until the peanut butter has melted. Bring to the boil, then simmer for 1 minute.

- Thread 2 strips of beef on each of the skewers, concertina fashion.

- Grill for 3 minutes each side until cooked through, brushing with any remaining marinade once or twice during cooking.

- Serve the skewers with the dipping sauce.

Makes 12 small cakes • Fusion • 🌙

Curried Fish Cakes

Preparation time:
15 minutes
Cooking time:
4–6 minutes
Freezeable for:
2 months, but best eaten fresh

These aren't traditional Thai fishcakes but they are really economical and taste excellent. As a quick and easy alternative, you can use a drained can of pink salmon, skin removed, or 120g seafood sticks, well mashed, instead of the tuna.

- Either peel the potatoes, cut into small chunks and boil in water until tender (about 10 minutes) or scrub, prick all over with a fork, wrap each in a piece of kitchen paper and microwave for about 7 minutes until soft. Leave to cool slightly, then peel.

- Place the cooked potato in a bowl, add the fish and mash thoroughly together, then add the spring onions, fish sauce, lemongrass, ginger and basil. Moisten with the milk, if necessary, then add a little of the beaten egg to bind the mixture together.

- Shape the mixture into 12 small cakes. Dip in the remaining egg, then the breadcrumbs to coat completely.

- Heat about 5mm sunflower oil in a large frying pan, and shallow-fry the cakes for 2–3 minutes on each side until golden brown. Drain on kitchen paper.

- Serve warm, garnished with rocket leaves and lime wedges, with sweet chilli sauce on the side.

Ingredients:
2 potatoes (or 350g cooked potato)
185g can tuna, drained
2 spring onions, finely chopped
1 tbsp Thai fish sauce
1 tbsp Thai green curry paste
1 tsp finely chopped lemongrass (or lemongrass purée)
1 tsp grated fresh root ginger (or ginger purée)
½ tsp dried basil
1 tbsp milk (optional)
1 egg, beaten
60g natural dried breadcrumbs
Sunflower oil

To garnish
Rocket leaves and lime wedges

To serve
Sweet Chilli Dipping Sauce (page 145) or use bought

Fish Curries

Apart from those made with prawns, fish curries aren't as popular in Britain as elsewhere in the world, which is a shame because the tender succulence of fish and its sensational taste-of-the-ocean flavour, blended with those fragrant and sometimes fiery spices, create magical combinations. In the next few pages, I hope to inspire you.

Always make sure you buy fish from sustainable sources that have been responsibly fished. They are now clearly marked in reputable fishmongers and on supermarket packs. This is vital if we want to preserve our fish for future generations as so many species have been over-fished, or caught in such a way that they destroy other marine life at the same time, or endanger habitats. That said, fish are extremely good for you and here I'll introduce you to some taste-tingling recipes to get you eating more (of the right kind of) fish every week!

CHAPTER 6

Preparation time:
10 minutes plus marinating
Cooking time:
15 minutes
Not suitable for freezing

Serves 4 • Indian • ♪

Tandoori Fish

Ingredients:
4 x 150g pieces haddock
    loin (or other meaty white
    fish)
90ml thick plain yoghurt
1 tbsp lemon juice
1 tsp ground cumin
1 tsp ground coriander
1 tbsp sweet paprika
½ tsp ground turmeric
¼ tsp chilli powder
A good pinch of salt
A little oil for greasing
To garnish
A few torn fresh coriander
    leaves
Lemon or lime wedges

To serve
Baked Mushroom Pilau Rice
    (page 131)
Spiced Green Salad (page
    142)

Try to use sustainable fish, preferably line-caught, and put the rice in the oven to cook before you bake the fish. Choose good, meaty fillets so they can absorb the flavours, stay moist and not fall apart when cooked. You can use 2 tbsp tandoori paste or powder instead of the spices for speed.

- Lay the fish in a shallow dish that will take it in one layer. Mix together the yoghurt, lemon juice, spices and salt and spoon over the fish. Turn the fish over in the mixture to coat completely, then leave to marinate for 1 hour in the fridge.

- Preheat the oven to 220°C/Gas 7 and oil a baking tin.

- Drain the fish and place in the prepared tin. Bake the fish in the oven for 15 minutes until cooked through and just browning.

- Transfer the fish to warm plates using a fish slice and garnish with a few torn coriander leaves and lemon or lime wedges. Spoon the juices from the baking tin over the rice to serve with the fish and a green salad.

Curried Prawn Orzotto

Preparation time:
15 minutes
Cooking time:
40 minutes
Freezeable for:
2 months

This is a favourite of mine that I keep tweaking and improving – this version has a bit more heat and more of a Thai flavour than earlier versions. Pearl barley makes a great risotto-style dish (orzo is barley in Italian) as it keeps its texture and the liquid can be added all in one go.

- Heat the oil in a large saucepan. Add the spring onions, garlic and diced pepper and fry, stirring, for 1 minute.

- Stir in the turmeric, curry paste and chopped chilli and cook for a further 30 seconds. Stir in the barley until the grains are glistening, then add the coconut milk, stock and fish sauce. Bring to the boil, reduce the heat, and simmer, gently for 35 minutes.

- Add the prawns, stir well and cook for a further 5 minutes until they're pink and the barley has absorbed most of the liquid and is tender but still with bite.

- Meanwhile, blanch the mangetout in a little boiling water for 1 minute until just tender. Drain. Add to the orzotto, toss gently and serve in bowls, garnished with the torn herbs and wedges of lime, if liked.

Ingredients:
2 tbsp sunflower oil
1 bunch of spring onions, chopped
1 garlic clove, crushed (or ½ tsp garlic purée)
1 red pepper, diced
1 tsp ground turmeric
1 tbsp Thai red curry paste
1 fat red chilli, deseeded, if liked, and finely chopped
200g pearl barley
400ml can of coconut milk
300ml chicken stock
1 tbsp Thai fish sauce
400g raw peeled king prawns
100g mangetout, trimmed and chopped
Salt and freshly ground black pepper

To garnish
2 tbsp torn fresh coriander, flatleaf parsley or basil leaves
Lime wedges

Preparation time:
20 minutes
Cooking time:
28 minutes
Freezable for:
1 month, but best eaten fresh

Serves 4 • Caribbean • ♪♪

West Indian-style Prawn Curry with Fresh Pineapple

Ingredients:
1 small fresh pineapple
2 tbsp sunflower oil
1 large onion, finely chopped (or 2 handfuls of frozen chopped onion)
1 large garlic clove, finely chopped (or 1 tsp garlic purée)
1 tsp grated fresh root ginger (or ginger purée)
2 tsp black mustard seeds
1 tsp ground cumin
1 tsp ground turmeric
1–2 tsp crushed dried chillies
½ tsp ground coriander
1 thin red chilli, deseeded, if liked, and finely chopped
1 beefsteak tomato, skinned and chopped
1 red pepper, diced
2 tsp tomato purée
200ml vegetable stock
Salt and freshly ground black pepper
400g raw peeled king prawns
2 tsp lime juice
1 tbsp chopped fresh or frozen coriander
To garnish
A few torn coriander leaves (optional)
Lime wedges
To serve
Plain Basmati Rice (page 128)
Green salad

The sweet/sharp flavour of fresh pineapple blends beautifully with succulent prawns. You could use canned pineapple in natural juice if necessary but the flavour and texture won't be as good. For extra substance, add some cooked baby potatoes with the prawns.

- Top and tail the pineapple, stand it upright and cut off all the skin in downward slices. Halve the pineapple, remove the thick central core, then cut in cubes. Set aside.

- Heat the oil in a saucepan, add the onion and fry, stirring, for 2 minutes until softened but not browned.

- Add the garlic, ginger and spices and fry, stirring, until the mustard seeds start to 'pop'.

- Add the tomato, pepper, tomato purée, stock and salt and pepper to taste. Bring to the boil and simmer for 15 minutes until the sauce has thickened slightly.

- Add the pineapple and prawns and simmer for about a further 10 minutes.

- Add the lime juice and coriander, taste and re-season if necessary. Spoon over rice, garnish with a few torn coriander leaves and some wedges of lime and serve hot with a green salad.

Serves 4 • Indian • ☽

Quick Prawn and Pea Curry

Preparation time:
10 minutes
Cooking time:
17 minutes
Not suitable for freezing

Keep a bag of cooked peeled cold water prawns in the freezer – they are great for making a last-minute curry when time is short. Don't overcook them, though, or they'll go tough and shrink. I've included peas here to give a complete dish – great for a TV supper.

- Heat the oil in a large saucepan. Add the onion and fry, stirring, for 3–4 minutes until lightly golden.

- Stir in the curry powder and cook, stirring, for 30 seconds. Add the remaining ingredients except the prawns and half the coriander. Bring to the boil, then reduce the heat and simmer very gently for 5–10 minutes until thick.

- Stir in the prawns and half the coriander and simmer, stirring gently, for 2–3 minutes until the prawns are hot through. Taste and re-season if necessary.

- Serve on a bed of rice, garnished with tomatoes and cucumber.

Ingredients:
2 tbsp sunflower oil
1 large onion chopped (or 2 large handfuls of frozen chopped onion)
3 tbsp Madras curry powder
1 tbsp lemon or lime juice
1 garlic clove, crushed (or ½ tsp garlic purée)
2 tsp garam masala
½ tsp salt
400g can of chopped tomatoes
1 tbsp tomato purée
4 tbsp desiccated coconut
2 tsp soft light brown sugar
120ml water
175g frozen peas, thawed
400g cooked, peeled cold water prawns, thawed if frozen
2 tbsp chopped fresh or frozen coriander

To garnish
Tomato wedges and slices of cucumber

To serve
Plain Basmati Rice (page 128)

Preparation time:
10 minutes
Cooking time:
10 minutes
Not suitable for freezing

Serves 4 • Asian • ♪♪

Thai Green Fish Curry with Courgettes

Ingredients:
4 courgettes, cut into fingers
2 tbsp Thai green curry paste
1 fat green chilli, seeded and
   cut into thin strips
1 tsp finely chopped
   lemongrass (or lemongrass
   purée)
2 kaffir lime leaves
2 tbsp Thai fish sauce
400ml can of coconut milk
Salt and freshly ground black
   pepper
600g thick salmon fillet,
   skinned and cut into large
   chunks

To garnish
A few torn coriander leaves
Lime wedges

To serve
Perfect Thai Jasmine Rice
   (page 129)

Although this is usually made with white fish, it is delicious made with salmon – but choose thick steaks rather than thin fillets from the tail end. Of course, use chunky, white sustainable fish, such as coley, instead if you prefer.

- Blanch the courgettes in boiling water for 3 minutes, drain, rinse with cold water and drain again.

- Mix the curry paste, chilli, lemongrass, kaffir lime leaves, fish sauce and coconut milk together in a large saucepan. Stir in the salmon. Bring to the boil, reduce the heat, part-cover and simmer gently for 5 minutes. Stir in the courgettes and heat through for 2 minutes.

- Discard the lime leaves and serve spooned over jasmine rice in bowls, garnished with a few torn coriander leaves and a wedge of lime in each bowl.

Curried Salt Fish Stew with Potatoes and Peppers

Preparation time:
15 minutes plus soaking
Cooking time:
40 minutes
Not suitable for freezing

This is a fusion between Portugal and the Caribbean! It's loosely based on a recipe I had from Trinidad but I added peppers and tomatoes and substituted cold water prawns instead of the fatter, warm water variety in the original.

- Soak the fish according to packet directions, changing the water at least once (even if the instructions don't tell you to). Drain and cut in chunks, discarding any bones.

- Heat the butter and oil in a large saucepan. Add the onions and fry, stirring, for 3 minutes until softened but not browned.

- Add the garlic and curry powder or paste and fry for 30 seconds. Add the peppers, potato, chilli, tomatoes, sugar, water and a good grinding of pepper. Bring to the boil, reduce the heat, cover and simmer for 25 minutes.

- Add the pieces of cod and simmer for a further 10 minutes until tender.

- Stir in the prawns and lime juice and heat through for a minute or two. Taste and add more sugar or lime juice to taste.

- Serve hot in large bowls with crusty bread or plain basmati rice, and a green salad.

Ingredients:
300g salt cod or pollack fillet
Large knob of butter
2 tbsp olive oil
2 onions, chopped (or 2 large handfuls of frozen chopped onion)
2 garlic cloves, crushed (or 1 tsp garlic purée)
3 tbsp Madras curry powder or paste
1 red pepper, halved, deseeded and cut in chunks
1 green pepper, halved, deseeded and cut in chunks
2 large potatoes, peeled and cut in small chunks
1 fat green chilli, deseeded, if liked, and finely chopped
400g can of chopped tomatoes
1 tsp soft light brown sugar
100ml water
Freshly ground black pepper
150g cooked, peeled cold water prawns, thawed, if frozen
1 tbsp lime juice

To serve
Crusty bread or Plain Basmati Rice (page 128)
Green salad

Preparation time:
25 minutes
Cooking time:
20 minutes
Freezable for:
3 months

Serves 4 • African • 𝄞𝄞

African-style Curried Fish Pot

Ingredients:
Large knob of butter
1 tbsp sunflower oil
1 onion, chopped (or a large
handful of frozen chopped
onion)
2 garlic cloves, crushed (or
1 tsp garlic purée)
2 tsp crushed chilli flakes
1 tsp ground coriander
1 tsp ground turmeric
½ tsp ground cinnamon
1 tbsp lime juice
1 tsp tamarind paste
1 green pepper, halved,
deseeded and thinly sliced
1 small aubergine, diced
1 fat red chilli, deseeded, if
liked, and finely chopped
400g can of chopped tomatoes
400ml can of coconut milk
410g can of butter beans,
drained
300ml fish, chicken or
vegetable stock
Salt and freshly ground black
pepper
500g white fish fillets, such
as pollack or coley, skinned
and cut in chunks

To garnish
A few torn coriander leaves

To serve
Plain Basmati Rice (page 128)

This curry is really more of a delicious main meal soup because it creates a lot of tasty broth as it cooks, rich and aromatic. It is therefore usually served in a deep bowl, spooned over plenty of plain basmati rice to soak it all up.

• Heat the butter and oil in a large saucepan, add the onion and fry for 3 minutes, stirring, until softened and just colouring.

• Stir in the garlic and all the spices, the lime juice and tamarind paste and fry for 1 minute.

• Add the pepper, aubergine, chilli, tomatoes, coconut milk, beans and stock, then bring to the boil. Season to taste with salt and pepper. Reduce the heat, part-cover and simmer for 15 minutes until the vegetables are tender.

• Add the fish and cook for 5 minutes.

• Taste and re-season. Serve spooned over rice in large soup bowls. Garnish with a few torn coriander leaves and eat with a spoon.

• Fish Curries

Curried Miso Grilled Salmon

Preparation time:
10 minutes plus marinating
Cooking time:
8 minutes
Not suitable for freezing

A superb fusion dish, this is a twist on teryiaki salmon. To the sweet and salty miso paste, instead of the traditional mirin or sherry, I've added curry paste and chilli, which gives added depth of flavour and makes for a really interesting dish.

- Mix the garlic, sugar, miso paste, curry powder, chilli, soy sauce and lime juice in a large, shallow, non-metallic dish. Add the salmon and turn it over to coat completely in the mixture. Leave to marinate for at least 2 hours, if possible.

- When nearly ready to serve, preheat the grill. Line the grill rack with oiled foil.

- Lay the fish, skin-side up on the foil and grill for 3 minutes.

- Carefully turn the fish over and grill for a further 5 minutes until cooked through and browning on top.

- Meanwhile, heat the noodles according to the packet directions. Drain, return them to the pan and toss in the oil and sesame seeds.

- Pile the noodles on plates, top with the salmon and serve with the beansprout salad.

Ingredients:
1 large garlic clove, crushed (or 1 tsp garlic purée)
1 tbsp soft light brown sugar
2 tbsp red or white miso paste
2 tbsp Madras curry paste
1 fat red chilli, deseeded, if liked, and finely chopped
1 tbsp soy sauce
1 tbsp lime juice
4 salmon steaks, about 150g each
2 tbsp sunflower oil
300g straight-to-wok thick udon noodles
1 tbsp sesame oil (or sunflower oil), plus a little for greasing
2 tbsp sesame seeds

To serve
Beansprout and Black Mustard Seed Salad (page 143)

Preparation time:
40 minutes
Cooking time:
9 minutes
Not suitable for freezing

Serves 4 • Asian • 🌙

Thai Green Curried Mussels

Ingredients:
Large knob of butter
1 tbsp sunflower oil
2 shallots, finely chopped
    (or 2 tbsp chopped frozen
    shallot)
2 celery sticks, finely
    chopped
1 large garlic clove, crushed
    (or 1 tsp garlic purée)
1 tsp grated fresh root
    ginger (or ginger purée)
3 tbsp Thai green curry paste
1 tbsp Thai fish sauce
2 fat green chillies,
    deseeded and shredded
400ml can of coconut milk
1kg fresh mussels, cleaned
    and de-bearded,
    discarding any broken or
    open ones

To garnish
2 tbsp chopped fresh
    coriander
1 lime, cut in wedges

To serve
Crusty bread
Thai-style Green Salad (page
    139)

If you have time, put the mussels in a large bowl, cover with cold water and sprinkle with some porridge oats, then leave for a couple of hours to help them self-clean before you rinse and then cook them. Use an onion instead of the shallots if you prefer.

• Heat the butter and oil in a large saucepan. Add the shallots and celery and fry gently, stirring, for 3 minutes until softened but not browned.

• Stir in the remaining ingredients except the mussels.

• When thoroughly blended, add the mussels. Bring to the boil, cover, reduce the heat and cook for 5 minutes. Discard any mussels that remain closed.

• Serve in large bowls, sprinkled with the chopped coriander, with lime wedges to squeeze over, crusty bread and a green salad.

Serves 4 • British • ♪

Kedgeree

Preparation time:
10 minutes
Cooking time:
12 minutes
Not suitable for freezing

This mild curried rice dish was introduced to England by British Colonials returning from India. It was eaten by Victorians for breakfast but makes a delicious lunch or supper dish – or is great to serve for brunch!

Ingredients:
350g long-grain rice
Salt and freshly ground black pepper
2 eggs, scrubbed and wrapped in foil
350g smoked haddock fillet
90g frozen peas
Large knob of butter
1 large onion, chopped (or 2 large handfuls of frozen chopped onion)
2 tsp Madras curry powder or paste
½ tsp garam masala
4 tbsp double cream
2 tbsp chopped fresh parsley
A little freshly grated nutmeg (optional)

- Bring a pan of lightly salted water to the boil. Add the rice, stir, add the eggs, bring back to the boil and boil for 5 minutes.

- Add the fish and peas and cook for a further 5 minutes.

- Carefully lift out the fish with a fish slice and place on a plate. Lift out the eggs and plunge in cold water. Drain the rice and peas.

- Flake the fish, discarding any skin and bones. Shell the eggs and cut into wedges.

- Meanwhile, melt the butter in a large pan. Add the onion, cover and fry gently for about 5 minutes until soft and lightly golden, stirring occasionally.

- Stir in the curry powder or paste and garam masala and cook for 1 minute, stirring.

- Add the rice and peas and mix well. Fold in the fish, cream and parsley and heat through, stirring and folding gently. Season to taste with salt, pepper and the nutmeg, if using.

- Pile onto plates and garnish each one with a few wedges of hard-boiled egg.

Chicken and Other Poultry Curries

Chicken is obviously the most common bird to use for curries but here you'll find a few duck, turkey and game recipes to try, too. The skill with poultry is not to overcook it or it becomes dry, even if it is cooked in lots of liquid, and the results can be stringy. It must be cooked through but that's all. So chicken curries are good ones to choose when you haven't much time as they cook more quickly (although some still benefit from marinating first if you can find the time).

For most of the curries, the skin is removed before cooking – which is good for the heart and good for the curry as the spices can permeate the flesh much more effectively. The exception is the duck, where the skin adds exceptional flavour (and the excess fat is poured off after browning to release it, anyway).

CHAPTER 7

Preparation time:
15 minutes
Cooking time:
40 minutes
Freezable for:
2 months

Serves 4 • Indian • ♪♪

Chicken and Red Lentil Curry

Ingredients:

2 tbsp sunflower oil
1 onion, chopped (or a large
  handful frozen chopped
  onion)
1 large garlic clove, crushed
  (or 1 tsp garlic purée)
2 large potatoes, peeled and
  cut in bite-sized chunks
1 thin red chilli, deseeded, if
  liked, and chopped
½ tsp chilli powder
1 tsp ground turmeric
2 tsp ground cumin
1 tsp ground coriander
½ tsp ground fenugreek
¼ tsp ground cloves
150g red lentils
400g skinless chicken breast,
  diced
2 tbsp malt or wine vinegar
400g can of chopped
  tomatoes
400ml chicken stock
1 tbsp smooth mango
  chutney
Salt and freshly ground black
  pepper
2 tsp garam masala
2 tbsp chopped fresh or
  frozen coriander

To serve
Plain Basmati Rice (page 128)
Spiced Green Salad (page 142)

There are many versions of this lentil-based dhanzak. This one is very simple to make but has a good flavour. You can make it with king prawns in exactly the same way but add the prawns for the last 5 minutes' cooking, just until they turn pink.

- Heat the oil in a large heavy-based saucepan and fry the onion and garlic, stirring for 1 minute.
- Add the potatoes and stir a further minute.
- Stir in the spices and cook, stirring for 1 minute.
- Add the lentils, chicken, vinegar, tomatoes, stock, mango chutney and some seasoning. Stir well. Bring back to the boil, reduce the heat, cover and simmer gently for 30 minutes.
- Add the garam masala and simmer a further minute. Taste and re-season if necessary. The sauce should be thick but not stodgy so thin, if necessary, with a little boiling water. Stir in the coriander.
- Spoon over plain basmati rice and serve with the green salad.

Chicken Biryani

Preparation time:
20 minutes
Cooking time:
40 minutes
Freezeable for:
3 months

If you have any cooked leftover chicken, or lamb, you can use that instead. Simply dice and add to the onions, omit the stock, add the spices and yoghurt, then simmer for 20 minutes until the sauce is thick. Finally add the cooked rice and continue as in the recipe.

- Heat the oil in a large saucepan. Add the onions and fry for about 5 minutes, stirring until soft and golden. Remove half and reserve for garnish.

- Add the chicken to the remaining onion and brown on all sides.

- Add all the spices, the bay leaf, and a little salt and pepper. Cook, stirring, for 1 minute.

- Stir in the yoghurt and the stock. Bring to the boil, reduce the heat, cover and simmer gently for 20 minutes.

- Remove the lid and continue to simmer, stirring occasionally, for a further 5–10 minutes until the liquid has evaporated and the chicken is tender and bathed in a rich sauce.

- Meanwhile, cook the rice in boiling, salted water for 10 minutes, adding the peas half way through cooking. Drain and return to the pan.

- Add the chicken to the rice, stir well. Taste and re-season, if necessary.

- Meanwhile reheat the extra fried onions and stir in the dried fruit and nuts. Spoon the biryani on to plates, garnish with the fruit and nut mixture, and serve with popadoms, the salad and carrot raita.

Ingredients:
2 tbsp sunflower oil
2 large onions, sliced
500g skinless chicken breast, diced
1 tsp grated fresh root ginger (or ginger purée)
1 garlic clove, crushed (or ½ tsp garlic purée)
¼ tsp chilli powder
1 tsp ground cumin
½ tsp ground coriander
½ tsp ground turmeric
1 bay leaf
200ml plain yoghurt
200ml chicken stock
Salt and freshly ground black pepper
350g basmati rice
100g frozen peas

To garnish
2 tbsp currants
2 tbsp toasted flaked almonds

To serve
Popadoms (page 134)
Carrot Raita (page 136)
Mixed Salad with Cumin and Onion Seed Dressing (page 141)

Cooking time:
15–20 minutes
Freezable for:
3 months

Chicken Tikka Masala

Ingredients:
For the marinade
1 tsp dried mint
1 onion, grated
1 large garlic clove, crushed
   (or 1 tsp garlic puree)
1 tsp grated fresh root
   ginger (or ginger purée)
1 fat green chilli, deseeded,
   if preferred, and roughly
   chopped
1 tsp ground coriander
1 tsp ground cumin
½ tsp ground turmeric
1 tsp garam masala
1 tbsp sweet paprika
2 tsp soft light brown sugar
1 tbsp lime juice
2 tbsp tomato purée
1 tsp salt
1 tbsp sunflower oil
250ml thick, creamy plain
   yoghurt

For the chicken
600g skinless chicken breast,
   diced
150ml water
2 tbsp ground almonds
120ml double cream
Lemon wedges, to garnish

To serve
Plain Basmati Rice (page
   128) or naan bread
Crisp green salad

I have created many versions of this dish, but this is made in the traditional way: the chicken is marinated, then grilled and added to a creamy, curry sauce made from the marinade. You could use 4 tbsp Chicken Tikka Masala paste instead and add to the yoghurt instead of the individual marinade ingredients.

- Mix all the ingredients for the marinade in a large bowl. Add the chicken, stir well and leave to marinate for at least 2 hours (or all day if necessary). If you are using wooden skewers, put them in a bowl of water to soak.

- Preheat the grill. Remove the chicken from the marinade, drain well and thread on metal or soaked wooden skewers. Grill for 10–15 minutes, turning once, until cooked through and slightly charred in places.

- Meanwhile, put the marinade in a pan with the water, almonds and cream. Bring to the boil, stirring until you have a thick, rich sauce.

- Remove all the chicken from the skewers and stir into the sauce. Simmer for a couple of minutes. Taste and re-season, if necessary.

- Serve with plain basmati rice or naan bread and a crisp green salad.

Preparation time:
10 minutes plus marinating
Cooking time:
25 minutes
Freezeable for:
3 months

Sautéed Chicken in Tomato Curry Sauce

This is my version of *murghi bhuna masala*. The chicken is marinated in the spices, garlic and onion, then sautéed in a mixture of butter or ghee and oil and finally simmered with tomatoes to form a rich and mouth-watering sauce.

- Mix the onion and garlic with all the spices. Add the chicken, mix well and leave to marinate for at least 2 hours or, preferably, all day or overnight.

- Heat the oil and butter or ghee in a large, deep frying pan. Add the chicken and brown quickly all over. Turn down the heat, cover and fry for a further 5 minutes until cooked through.

- Add the tomatoes and a good grinding of pepper. Bring to the boil, reduce the heat and simmer gently for about 15 minutes until the chicken is bathed in sauce.

- Taste and re-season, if necessary. Spoon the curry over rice, sprinkle with the chopped coriander and serve with raita and mango chutney.

Ingredients:
2 large onions, finely chopped
  (or 4 handfuls of frozen
  chopped onion)
1 large garlic clove, crushed
  (or 1 tsp garlic purée)
3 fat green chillies, deseeded
  and finely chopped
1 tsp grated fresh root ginger
  (or ginger purée)
½ tsp ground turmeric
½ tsp salt
600g chicken breast, diced
2 tbsp sunflower oil
Large knob of butter or
  1 tbsp ghee
400g can of chopped
  tomatoes
Freshly ground black pepper

To garnish
2 tbsp chopped fresh
  coriander

To serve
Plain Basmati Rice (page 128)
Cucumber Raita (page 137)
Fresh Mango Chutney (page
  138) or use bought

Tandoori Chicken

tion time:
...minutes plus marinating and resting

Cooking time:
40 minutes

Freezable for:
1 month, uncooked in the marinade, only if fresh chicken is used (not thawed frozen)

Ingredients:
4 chicken portions, skin removed
120ml thick, plain yoghurt
1 large garlic cloves, crushed (or 1 tsp garlic purée)
1 tbsp garam masala
2 tsp tomato purée
1½ tbsp sweet paprika
2 tsp grated fresh root ginger (or ginger purée)
Salt and freshly ground black pepper

To garnish
Fresh coriander and lemon wedges

To serve
Baked Mushroom Pilau (page 131)
Fresh Mango Chutney (page 138) or use bought
Mixed salad

We always used to add a drop of red and yellow food colouring – as did many Indian restaurants – but I prefer to colour just with paprika and, sometimes, tomato purée now. You can use a teaspoonful of achiote, a natural spice that colours food bright orange, if you fancy experimenting!

- Make several slashes in the flesh of the chicken with a sharp knife.

- Mix the remaining main ingredients together in a large, shallow dish. Add the chicken and rub the mixture well into the slits. Cover the dish with clingfilm and marinate in the fridge for several hours or up to 24 hours, as convenient.

- Preheat the oven to 220°C/Gas 7.

- Drain the chicken and place in a roasting tin. Bake in the oven for about 40 minutes, basting occasionally, until well browned in places and the juices run clear when pierced with a skewer in the thickest part. (Meanwhile make the rice on page 131 and place in the oven with the chicken whilst it's cooking, and prepare the garnish.)

- When the chicken is cooked, remove from the oven, cover with foil and leave to rest in a warm place with the rice.

- Place the chicken on plates with the rice and garnish with the coriander and lemon wedges. Serve with mango chutney and a mixed salad.

Creamy Chicken Curry

Preparation time:
10 minutes
Cooking time:
1 hour
Freezeable for:
3 months

My version of *poona murghi* is a very mild baked chicken curry, cooked in a lovely rich, creamy sauce. You must use double cream for this or it may curdle. Cook the mushroom pilau to serve with it for a truly delicious meal. Use chunks of chicken instead of portions if you prefer.

- Preheat the oven to 180°C/Gas 4.

- Put all the ingredients except the chicken, flour and water in a flameproof casserole. Blend the flour and water together and stir in. Bring to the boil, stirring until thickened. Add the chicken.

- Cover and cook in the oven for 1 hour. (Meanwhile make the mushroom pilau rice and put in the oven to cook with the chicken.)

- Taste the chicken and re-season if necessary. Garnish with plenty of chopped coriander or mint and serve with the baked mushroom pilau and a crisp green salad.

To slow cook: Prepare as above but when boiling, tip in the slow cooker and cook on Low for 6 hours, then serve with pilau rice.

To pressure cook: Prepare as above but do not thicken or add the cream. Cook at High Pressure for 5 minutes. Reduce the pressure quickly under cold water. Carefully lift out the chicken. Blend the flour and water together and stir in. Bring to the boil, stirring and cook for 2 minutes. Stir in the cream.

Ingredients:
1 large garlic clove, crushed
(or 1 tsp garlic purée)
1 tsp grated fresh root ginger
(or 1 tsp ginger purée)
1 tsp sweet paprika
1 tsp ground turmeric
¼–½ tsp chilli powder
½ tsp salt
300ml chicken stock
300ml double cream
4 chicken portions, skin
removed
3 tbsp plain flour
3 tbsp water

To garnish
Handful of chopped fresh
coriander or mint

To serve
Baked Mushroom Pilau (page
131)
Crisp green salad

Preparation time:
10 minutes
Cooking time:
35 minutes
Freezable for:
3 months, without the garnish

Serves 4 • Asian • 🌶🌶

Thai Green Chicken Curry with Sesame Carrot Ribbons

Ingredients:
2 tbsp sunflower oil
1 bunch of spring onions,
    cut in short diagonal
    lengths
2 green peppers, diced
4 chicken portions halved
    (or 4 thighs and 4
    drumsticks), skin removed
4 tbsp Thai green curry paste
1 tsp finely chopped
    lemongrass (or lemongrass
    purée)
400ml can of coconut milk
1 tbsp Thai fish sauce
2 kaffir lime leaves
2 carrots
2 tsp sesame oil
1 tbsp toasted sesame seeds

To serve
Perfect Thai Jasmine Rice
    (page 129)
Thai-style Green Salad (page
    139)

I keep trying to come up with ways to improve this really simple dish so I've created a new, tasty garnish! You could just boil or steam the carrot ribbons for a minute and add them to the curry just before serving, if you prefer, or use diced chicken breast and cook for just 10 minutes.

- Heat half the oil in a saucepan. Add the spring onions and peppers and fry for 2 minutes, stirring. Remove with a slotted spoon.

- Heat the remaining oil, add the chicken and brown over a medium-high heat on all sides. Remove from the pan.

- Stir in the curry paste and lemongrass, then blend in the coconut milk and Thai fish sauce. Return the pepper, onions and chicken to the sauce. Tuck in the kaffir lime leaves. Bring back to the boil, reduce the heat, cover and simmer gently for 30 minutes until the chicken is really tender and cooked through. Discard the lime leaves.

- Meanwhile, peel or scrape the carrots and pare into ribbons with a potato peeler. Toss in the sesame oil and seeds.

- Spoon the cooked curry over jasmine rice in bowls, top with a little pile of the carrot ribbons and serve with a Thai-style green salad.

Preparation time:
25 minutes plus marinating
Cooking time:
35 minutes
Freezeable for:
3 months

Serves 4 • Indian • ♪♪♪

Hot and Sour Chicken Curry

Like the Goan pork curry on page 99, this is a fiery curry, similar to a chicken vindaloo. Use lamb, if you prefer, and reduce the heat by omitting the chilli powder if it suits your palate better. I've ground some spices for this paste but you can just grate the onion and use ground spices.

- In a dry frying pan, toast the cumin and mustard seeds for 30 seconds until fragrant. Tip into a mortar or a small food processor. Add the onion, chillies, cardamom seeds, ginger and garlic. Pound or blend to a paste, adding 1–2 tbsp of the vinegar. Add the chilli powder, cinnamon and turmeric.

- Spoon into a plastic container with a lid. Add the chicken and toss well with your hands so it is all well coated in the paste. Ideally, cover and leave to marinate for several hours (or overnight if that suits you better).

- Heat the oil in a large heavy-based pan. Add the chicken and marinade and fry, stirring, for 2–3 minutes.

- Add the tomatoes, the remaining vinegar, the water and a little salt. Bring to the boil, reduce the heat and simmer gently for about 30 minutes, stirring occasionally, until rich, thick and the chicken is tender. Taste and re-season, if necessary.

- Garnish with fresh coriander, if using, and serve with plain basmati rice, cucumber raita, a large mixed salad and mango chutney.

Ingredients:
2 tsp cumin seeds
1 tsp black mustard seeds
1 onion, roughly chopped
4 thin red chillies, deseeded, if liked, and chopped
4 cardamom pods, split, seeds extracted
2 tsp grated fresh root ginger (or ginger purée)
2 garlic cloves, chopped (or 1 tsp garlic purée)
90ml red wine vinegar
1 tsp chilli powder
1 tsp ground cinnamon
1 tsp ground turmeric
600g skinless chicken thigh meat, diced
2 tbsp sunflower oil
400g can of chopped tomatoes
200ml water
Salt

To garnish
Chopped fresh coriander (optional)

To serve
Plain Basmati Rice (page 128)
Carrot Raita (page 136)
Large mixed salad
Fresh Mango Chutney (page 138) or use bought

Japanese Chicken Curry

paration time:
10 minutes
Cooking time:
18 minutes
Not suitable for freezing

Ingredients:

1 tbsp sunflower oil
1 onion, chopped (or a large handful frozen chopped onion)
2 tbsp plain flour
300ml chicken stock
1 tbsp tomato purée
2 tsp Worcestershire sauce
2 tsp garam masala
¼ tsp chilli powder
1 eating apple, peeled, cored and grated
100g cup shiitake or cup mushrooms, thickly sliced
1 tsp caster sugar
350g cooked leftover chicken, cut in bite-sized pieces
12 pieces of cooked, waxy potatoes
4 heaped tbsp cooked, sliced carrots
2 heaped tbsp cooked peas
Salt and freshly ground black pepper

To serve
Plain Basmati Rice (page 128)

This is a great way to use up the leftover chicken on a Monday and is my version of a *katsu* curry, which is mild, sweet and thickened with a roux. If you don't have cooked leftover vegetables, simply cook them in boiling, lightly salted water until tender, then continue as in the recipe.

- Heat the oil in a large saucepan. Add the onion and fry, stirring, for 5 minutes until soft and lightly golden.

- Stir in the flour and cook, stirring, for 1 minute.

- Stir in the stock, bring to the boil and cook for 2 minutes, stirring until thickened.

- Add all the remaining ingredients. Bring back to the boil, reduce the heat, cover and simmer gently for 10 minutes until rich and thick, stirring gently occasionally.

- Taste and re-season if necessary. Serve on a bed of plain rice.

Yellow Ginger Chicken

Preparation time:
10 minutes
Cooking time:
15 minutes
Freezeable for:
3 months, without the cream,
nuts and coriander

The warmth of the ginger and the heat of the chillies in this recipe are softened with the addition of some cream added at the end of cooking. You could add some reduced-fat crème fraîche instead for a lighter finished dish but don't let it boil.

- Heat the oil in a saucepan, add the onion and fry, stirring, for 3 minutes to soften.

- Add the garlic and fry a further 1 minute.

- Stir in the spices and fry 30 seconds.

- Add the chicken and fry, stirring, for a few minutes until opaque.

- Stir in the coconut milk and fish sauce and season to taste with salt and pepper. Bring to the boil, reduce the heat, part-cover and simmer gently for 10 minutes until the chicken is tender and cooked through.

- Stir in the cream, taste and re-season, if necessary.

- Stir in half the nuts and coriander. Spoon over jasmine rice in bowls, sprinkle the remaining nuts and coriander and garnish each bowl with a lemon wedge.

Ingredients:
2 tbsp sunflower oil
1 large onion, chopped (or 2 large handfuls of frozen chopped onion)
2 garlic cloves, crushed (or 1 tsp garlic purée)
2 tsp ground turmeric
1 tbsp grated fresh root ginger (or ginger purée)
1 tsp ground cumin
2 tsp finely chopped lemongrass (or lemongrass purée)
2–3 thin red chillies, deseeded, if liked, and finely chopped
600g skinless chicken breast, diced
400ml can of coconut milk
1 tbsp Thai fish sauce
Salt and freshly ground black pepper
3 tbsp single cream
50g roasted unsalted cashew nuts, chopped
Handful of torn fresh coriander leaves

To garnish
4 lemon wedges

To serve
Perfect Thai Jasmine Rice (page 129)

Preparation time:
25 minutes
Cooking time:
1¼ hours
Freezable for:
3 months

Ingredients:
2 tbsp sunflower oil
1 bunch of spring onions,
    cut in short lengths
1 garlic clove, crushed (or
    ½ tsp garlic purée)
1 tsp ground turmeric
1 tbsp Madras curry powder
    or paste
500g skinless chicken breast,
    diced
400g can of green lentils,
    drained
150ml chicken stock
400ml can of coconut milk
1 small butternut squash,
    peeled, deseeded and cut
    into bite-sized chunks
1 red pepper, diced
Salt and freshly ground black
    pepper
2 tbsp toasted pumpkin
    seeds

To serve
Perfect Thai Jasmine Rice
    (page 129)
Caribbean Roti Breads (page
    135)
Mixed salad

Serves 4 • Fusion • ♪

Chicken and Butternut Squash Curry with Lentils

This is a bit of a hybrid. It has Caribbean and Thai influences but the result is a great-tasting, fairly thin curry that is delicious served with rice and/or roti breads and a large mixed salad, preferably with some avocado.

• Preheat the oven to 180°C/Gas 4.

• Heat the oil in a large flameproof casserole. Reserve some of the chopped green tops from the onions, add the rest of the green and the white parts to the casserole and fry, stirring, for 2 minutes.

• Stir in the garlic, spices and chicken and fry, stirring, for a few minutes until the chicken is opaque.

• Stir in the lentils, stock and coconut milk, then the butternut squash and pepper. Season and bring to the boil.

• Cover and place in the oven to cook for 1 hour until the chicken and vegetables are tender.

• Stir the curry, taste and re-season if necessary.

• Spoon into bowls, on rice, if liked, scatter the pumpkin seeds over, and serve with roti breads, if using, and a mixed salad.

To slow cook: Prepare as above but omit the stock. Bring to the boil, tip in the slow cooker and cook on Low for 6 hours.

To pressure cook: Prepare as above but omit the stock. Cook at High Pressure for 5 minutes. Reduce the pressure quickly under cold water.

• Chicken and Other Poultry Curries

Serves 4 • Asian • 🌙

Preparation time:
10 minutes
Cooking time:
15 minutes
Freezeable for:
3 months, before thickening

Chinese Chicken Curry with Baby Sweetcorn

Quick and simple, this makes a delicious midweek meal. You could substitute 400g thawed frozen cooked peeled prawns instead of the chicken but add them at the end and heat through for a few minutes before serving.

- Heat the oil in a wok or saucepan. Fry the spring onions, stirring, for 2 minutes until soft and lightly golden.

- Stir in the garlic and curry powder and fry for a further 30 seconds. Add the stock, honey and soy sauce. Stir well, then and add the chicken pieces and baby corn. Bring to the boil, reduce the heat, cover and simmer gently for 10 minutes until the chicken and corn are tender and cooked through.

- Blend the cornflour with the water and stir into the chicken. Bring to the boil, stirring, and simmer for 1 minute. Taste and add more soy sauce if necessary.

- Serve hot spooned over plain basmati rice in bowls.

Ingredients:
2 tbsp sunflower oil
1 bunch of spring onions, cut in short lengths
2 large garlic cloves, crushed (or 2 tsp garlic purée)
1 tbsp Madras curry powder
300ml chicken stock
2 tsp clear honey
3 tbsp soy sauce
600g skinless chicken breast, diced
100g baby sweetcorn, cut in short lengths
2 tbsp cornflour
2 tbsp water

To serve
Plain Basmati Rice (page 128)

Preparation time:
15 minutes plus marinating
Cooking time:
30 minutes, plus standing

Serves 4 • Asian • 🌶

Curried Chicken and Almond Pilaf

Ingredients:
200ml can of evaporated milk
2 tbsp tomato purée
2 garlic cloves, crushed (or
 1 tsp garlic purée)
1 fat green chilli, deseeded, if
 liked, and finely chopped
Grated zest and juice of 1
 lime
½ tsp salt
1 tsp ground cumin
1 tsp ground turmeric
1 piece of cinnamon stick
Seeds from 4 cardamom pods
2 star anise
1 tsp grated fresh root
 ginger (or ginger purée)
25g ground almonds
4 chicken legs and 4 chicken
 thighs, skin removed
350g basmati rice
25g butter or ghee
750ml hot chicken stock

For the garnish
1 tbsp sunflower oil
1 onion, halved and thinly
 sliced
Small handful of whole
 blanched almonds
Small handful of raisins
2 tbsp chopped fresh
 coriander

To serve
Small mixed salad

This is my take on *nasi bokhar*, a Malaysian rice dish. It has a wonderful flavour of sweet spices with a little kick of chilli but not too much. You can make it with lamb cutlets instead of the chicken and garnish with chopped mint instead of coriander.

- Mix the evaporated milk, tomato purée, garlic, chilli, lime zest and juice, the salt, all the spices and the ground almonds. Make several slashes in the chicken. Add to the marinade, turn to coat well and leave to marinate for at least 2 hours or preferably all day or overnight.

- Wash the rice well and drain thoroughly.

- Melt the butter in a large saucepan. Lift the chicken out of the marinade, add to the pan and fry quickly on all sides to brown, turn down the heat and fry for 10 minutes, turning once or twice. Remove from the pan.

- Add the rice and stir until all the grains are coated in the pan juices. Add the marinade and stock and bring to the boil. Return the chicken to the pan. Cover tightly with a lid, reduce the heat as low as possible and cook gently for 20 minutes.

- Meanwhile, to make the garnish, heat the oil in a frying pan, add the onion and fry, stirring, for 3 minutes until golden.

- Stir in the almonds and raisins and fry, stirring, just until the almonds are turning golden. Drain on kitchen paper.

- Remove the pilaf from the heat. Lift off the lid and allow the steam to escape for a couple of minutes. Remove the chicken and fluff up the rice. Spoon it on plates and top with the chicken, then garnish with the almonds and raisins and the chopped coriander.

- Serve with a mixed salad.

Chicken, Mango and Spiced Almond Salad

Preparation time:
15 minutes
Cooking time:
3 minutes
Not suitable for freezing

You can either roast a small, whole chicken for this recipe or buy a rotisserie chicken from your local supermarket (they can be a bit pricey but you can often get them reduced if you shop at the end of the day – and they do taste really good!).

- Cut the chicken in quarters, then each quarter in half at the joint to make 8 pieces. Peel the mango, cut the flesh off the stone then dice the flesh. Separate the lettuce into leaves, wash, pat dry, tear into pieces and arrange on a large platter. Put the piece of chicken on top and scatter the fresh mango around.

- To make the spiced almonds, melt the butter in a frying pan. Add the almonds and fry, stirring, for a few minutes until golden brown. Remove from the heat. Add the spices and salt and toss well until coated. Drain on kitchen paper.

- To make the dressing, mix all the dressing ingredients together and season to taste.

- Spoon the dressing over the chicken and sprinkle the almonds over. Serve with warm new potatoes.

Ingredients:
1 small ready-roasted chicken
   (about 1.2kg)
1 small mango
1 small round or curly-leaf
   lettuce

For the almonds
Large knob of butter
50g blanched almonds
¼ tsp chilli powder
¼ tsp mixed spice
¼ tsp salt

For the dressing
5 tbsp mayonnaise
5 tbsp crème fraîche
1 tbsp tomato purée
1 tbsp Worcestershire sauce
1 tbsp Madras curry powder
   or paste
5cm piece of cucumber,
   peeled and chopped
Freshly ground black pepper

To serve
Warm new potatoes

Preparation time:
20 minutes
Cooking time:
25 minutes
Freezable for:
3 months, without the omelette

Serves 4 • Asian • ♪

Turkey Curry with Shredded Egg and Pak Choi

Ingredients:
3 tbsp sunflower oil
500g turkey stir-fry meat (or turkey breast steaks, cut in strips)
400ml can of coconut milk
1 tbsp chopped fresh mint (or 1 tsp dried)
2 tbsp Thai red curry paste
1 tbsp Thai fish sauce
1 tsp grated fresh root ginger (or ginger purée)
1 thin red chilli, deseeded, if liked, and finely chopped
Salt and freshly ground black pepper
1 large garlic clove, finely chopped (or 1 tsp garlic purée)
2 pak choi, finely shredded
2 eggs, beaten

To garnish
A few torn coriander or flat parsley leaves

To serve
Rice noodles

Turkey makes a delicious change from chicken in many curries but this tastes particularly good in its own right, especially with the omelette (which is also good as a topping to some shredded turkey tossed with noodles and a splash of hoisin sauce and a some crushed dried chillies until piping hot).

- Heat 1 tbsp of the sunflower oil in a saucepan. Add the turkey and stir-fry for 2 minutes.

- Add the coconut milk, mint, curry paste, fish sauce, ginger and chilli. Bring to the boil, reduce the heat and simmer gently for 15 minutes until the turkey is really tender. Taste and re-season.

- Meanwhile, heat the remaining oil in a frying pan. Add the garlic and pak choi and stir-fry for 2 minutes until wilted and softened.

- Season the beaten eggs with a little salt and pepper. Spread out the pak choi in the pan. Pour in the beaten eggs. Cook, lifting and stirring to allow the egg to run underneath and set.

- When completely set and browned underneath, gently slide the omelette out onto a plate, then invert back into the pan to cook the other side. Roll up and slide onto a plate again and cut into shreds.

- Spoon the curry over rice noodles in large bowls and top each one with some of the pak choi omelette shreds. Serve hot.

Serves 4 • British • ♪

One Pot Turkey Lentil and Vegetable Curry

Preparation time:
15 minutes
Cooking time:
40 minutes
Not suitable for freezing

This is a throw-together-and-let-it-simmer, mild curried stew with plenty of added vegetables so you can serve it as a complete meal without extra vegetables. Use chicken instead of turkey if you prefer. Curry paste is better than powder for this.

- Heat the oil in a large saucepan. Fry the onion, leek and carrot for 2 minutes, stirring.

- Add the curry paste and ginger and fry for a further 30 seconds.

- Add the turkey and fry until opaque, stirring all the time. Add all the remaining ingredients except the peas, bring to the boil, reduce the heat and simmer gently for 40 minutes until everything is cooked.

- Add the peas and simmer uncovered for a further 5 minutes, stirring occasionally. Discard the bay leaf. Taste and re-season. Serve hot in bowls.

To slow cook: Prepare as above but use only 400ml stock. When you bring back to the boil, tip into the crock pot and cook on Low for 6–8 hours.

To pressure cook: Prepare as above but use only 400ml stock. Cook at High Pressure for 10 minutes. Reduce the pressure quickly under cold water.

Ingredients:
2 tbsp sunflower oil
1 onion, chopped (or a large handful frozen, chopped onion)
1 leek, thickly sliced
2 carrots, sliced
2–3 tbsp Madras curry paste
2 tsp grated fresh root ginger (or ginger purée)
600g turkey thigh meat, diced
4 potatoes, peeled and cut in chunks
2 tbsp tomato purée
1 tsp soft light brown sugar
100g creamed coconut
500ml chicken stock
100g red lentils
1 bay leaf
Salt and freshly ground black pepper
100g frozen peas

Preparation time:
25 minutes
Cooking time:
2 hours
Freezable for:
3 months

Serves 4 • Asian • ♪♪

Red Duck and Roasted Red Pepper Curry

Ingredients:
2 red peppers
1 small oven-ready duck, about 2 kg, cut into 8 pieces
4 tbsp Thai red curry paste
2 fat red chillies, deseeded and cut in thin strips
2 tsp finely chopped lemongrass (or lemongrass purée)
600ml chicken stock
100g creamed coconut
2 tbsp Thai fish sauce
12 cherry tomatoes, halved
Salt and freshly ground black pepper

To serve
Perfect Thai Jasmine Rice (page 129)
Stir-fried Mangetout and Spring Onions (page 125)

You can use 4 halved duck portions or 4 breasts with skin.

- Preheat the grill. Grill the peppers, turning occasionally, until blackened all over (about 15 minutes). Put the peppers in a plastic bag and leave to cool.

- Scrape off all the black skin, halve the peppers and remove the seeds. Rinse, pat dry, then cut into large dice.

- Preheat the oven to 160°C/Gas 3.

- Heat a large flameproof casserole. Fry the duck pieces skin-sides down until the fat runs then turn and brown the other sides. Remove from the casserole. Drain the fat and wipe out the pan.

- Stir in the remaining ingredients except the tomatoes. Bring to the boil, stirring until the coconut melts. Add the duck and peppers. If the duck is not covered with the sauce, add a little more stock.

- Cover the casserole and cook in the oven for 1¾ hours until the duck is really tender. Spoon off any fat.

- Add the cherry tomatoes and return to the oven for 5 minutes so they soften but still hold their shape. Taste and re-season.

- Spoon over rice and serve with mangetout and spring onions.

To slow cook: Use only 400ml chicken stock and cook on Low for 8–10 hours. Add the cherry tomatoes, cover and cook on HIGH for 5 minutes.

To pressure cook: Prepare as above but use only 400ml chicken stock. Cook at High Pressure for 10 minutes. Reduce the pressure quickly under cold water. Add the cherry tomatoes and simmer gently in the open pan for 2–3 minutes.

Serves 4 • British • 🌶

Curried Duck Breasts with Glazed Pears

Preparation time:
15 minutes plus marinating
Cooking time:
10 minutes
Not suitable for freezing

This is equally good with pigeon breasts, but you'll need two breasts per person and cook for 1–2 minutes each side only. The skill is to marinate the breasts for several hours then cook them quickly and let them rest so they are tender and succulent.

- Make several slashes in the duck breasts. Mix all the ingredients for the duck except 2 tbsp of the oil and the stock together in a large shallow dish. Add the duck and smear the paste all over, rubbing well into the slashes. Cover and chill in the fridge for at least 2 hours or all day, if necessary.

- Heat the 2 tbsp oil in a frying pan. Lift the duck out of the marinade, scraping off excess paste back into the container. Fry the breasts for 4 minutes on each side until golden on the outside but pink in the centre. Wrap in foil and keep warm.

- Pour off any fat in the frying pan. Add the stock to the remainder of the spice paste in the container, stir well then pour into the frying pan. Bring to the boil and boil rapidly, stirring, for 1–2 minutes until thickened slightly. Taste and re-season if necessary.

- Meanwhile, put the pear quarters in a shallow pan with the apple juice, star anise and cinnamon stick. Bring to the boil, cover, reduce the heat and simmer gently for 5 minutes, then remove the lid, turn up the heat to moderate and let the mixture bubble for several minutes until the apple juice has almost evaporated and the fruit is soft but still holds its shape.

- Cut the duck breasts into thick diagonal slices. Arrange on top of bowls of rice. Spoon the sauce over then garnish each bowl with two spiced pear quarters (discarding the spices) and a sprig of parsley. Serve with the mixed salad.

Ingredients:

For the duck
4 skinless duck breasts
2 fat red chillies, deseeded, if liked, and finely chopped
1 large garlic clove, crushed (or 1 tsp garlic purée)
1 tsp grated fresh root ginger (or 1 tsp garlic purée)
2 tbsp tomato purée
1 tbsp tamarind paste
1 tbsp sweet paprika
1 tsp ground cumin
½ tsp ground turmeric
½ tsp ground cloves
4 cardamom pods, split, seeds extracted
1 tbsp soft light brown sugar
¼ tsp salt
4 tbsp sunflower oil
250ml chicken stock

For the pears
2 firm pears, halved, cored and quartered
100ml cloudy apple juice
1 star anise
1 piece of cinnamon stick
4 parsley sprigs, to garnish

To serve
Plain Basmati Rice (page 128)
Mixed Salad with Cumin and Onion Seed Dressing (page 141)

Beef Curries

There are two types of beef curry – those that need long, slow cooking to tenderise cheaper cuts of stewing or braising steak, and others quickly cooked using thin strips of more tender meat, like frying, rump or fillet steak. Many beef curries are versions of chicken or lamb ones in other chapters so, rather than duplicate, I created some different curries for you to try (along with a few classics, of course). There is something for every occasion here, from quick after-work or family suppers to speciality dishes perfect for entertaining. Beef has a good, robust flavour and texture so can take on board any number of spicy combinations with ease. The longer-cooking curries benefit from cooking then reheating the next day to get the full impact of the complex tastes. Most would be good with lamb, goat or even venison to add variation to your spicy repertoire. By the way, many people mistakenly believe that beef is not used in Indian cooking but, in fact, beef curries are very popular in Southern India.

CHAPTER 8

Preparation time:
20 minutes
Cooking time:
20 minutes
Freezable for:
2 months, without the tomatoes

Serves 4 • Indian • ♪

Minced Beef Curry with Broad Beans

Ingredients:
175g baby broad beans
2 tbsp sunflower oil
1 large onion, chopped (or a large handful frozen chopped)
2 garlic cloves, crushed (or 1 tsp garlic purée)
500g lean minced beef
1–2 tbsp Madras curry powder or paste
2 tsp grated fresh root ginger (or ginger purée)
300ml beef stock
1 tbsp tomato purée

To serve
Plain Basmati Rice (page 128)
Green salad

I've done keema recipes before adding peas to the mix but I've discovered that it's also absolutely delicious with a load of baby broad beans added at the last minute. Removing the skins from the broad beans is not vital – but is worth the effort!

• Boil the beans in lightly salted water for about 6 minutes or until tender. Drain, rinse with cold water then pop each bean out of its skin (not vital but nicer). Set aside.

• Heat the oil in a large saucepan. Add the onions and garlic and fry gently, stirring, for 3 minutes until softened but not browned.

• Add the minced beef and fry, stirring, until it is no longer pink and all the grains are separate.

• Stir in the curry powder or paste and fry for a further 1 minute, stirring.

• Add the ginger, stock and tomato purée. Bring to the boil stirring, reduce the heat and simmer gently for 15 minutes, stirring from time to time.

• Add the baby beans, cover and simmer a further 5 minutes. Stir gently to mix everything together. Season to taste with salt.

• Serve spooned over basmati rice with mango chutney and a crisp green salad.

• Beef Curries

Serves 4 • Indian • 🌶

Preparation time:
15 minutes
Cooking time:
20 minutes
Freezeable for:
3 months

Curried Beef with Mushrooms and Raisins

A quick beef curry for when time is short, this is also good made with chicken, in which case use 4 small skinless chicken breasts, cut into nice thin slices, instead of the frying steak. You can use any sort of mushrooms.

- Put the steak in a plastic bag and beat with a meat mallet or rolling pin to flatten and tenderise slightly. Cut in thin strips.
- Heat the oil in a saucepan. Add the onion and garlic and fry, stirring, for 2 minutes until softened but not browned.
- Add the beef, all the spices and the mushrooms and cook, stirring, until the meat is browned on all sides.
- Add the stock, raisins and sugar, part-cover and simmer for 10 minutes.
- Add the peas and sprinkle with a little salt. Re-cover and cook for about 10 minutes, stirring occasionally, until the beef and peas are tender and the sauce has reduced slightly. Taste and re-season if necessary.
- Serve with plain basmati rice and a carrot and beetroot salad.

Ingredients:
450g beef frying steak
1 tbsp sunflower oil
1 onion, chopped (or a large handful of frozen chopped)
1 garlic clove, crushed (or ½ tsp garlic purée)
1 tsp grated fresh root ginger (or ginger purée)
2 tbsp Madras curry powder or paste
2 tsp sweet paprika
1½ tsp ground cinnamon
100g mushrooms, sliced
300ml beef stock
Handful of raisins
1 tsp caster sugar
150g frozen peas
Salt

To serve
Plain Basmati Rice (page 128)
Carrot and Beetroot Salad with Mustard Yoghurt Dressing (page 140)

Preparation time:
15 minutes
Cooking time:
30 minutes
Freezable for:
3 months

Serves 4 • Fusion • ♪♪

Curry con Carne

Ingredients:

1 tbsp sunflower oil

1 onion, chopped (or 1 large handful frozen chopped onion)

1 garlic clove, crushed (or ½ tsp garlic purée)

450g lean minced beef

2 tbsp Madras curry powder

1 tsp ground cumin

½ tsp chilli powder

½ tsp soft light brown sugar

1 tsp dried oregano

400g can of pinto beans, drained

400g can of chopped tomatoes

2 tbsp tomato purée

150ml beef stock

2 tbsp chopped pickled jalapeño peppers

Salt and freshly ground black pepper

3 ripe avocados

2 tsp lime juice

To garnish

A little chopped fresh coriander

To serve

Plain Basmati Rice (page 128), flour tortillas or naan breads

Green salad

A variation on Mexican or Texas chilli con carne, you get the fire from the chillies, the mellow flavour from the curry and the fragrance of the oregano – a winning combination. I've served it with a basic guacamole – simply ripe avocado crushed with some lime juice.

• Heat the oil in a large saucepan. Add the onion, garlic and beef and fry, stirring, until the grains of meat are separate and no longer pink.

• Stir in the curry powder, cumin and chilli and fry, stirring, for 30 seconds. Add all the remaining ingredients except the avocados and lime juice. Bring to the boil, reduce the heat and simmer for about 30 minutes until tender and bathed in a rich sauce, stirring occasionally. Taste and re-season.

• Meanwhile, halve, peel, stone and crush the avocados with the lime juice and a good grinding of black pepper.

• When the curry is cooked, spoon into bowls over plain rice, if using, and top each bowl with a good dollop of the crushed avocado. Sprinkle with the chopped coriander. Serve with flour tortillas or naans, if using, and a green salad.

To slow cook: Prepare as above but omit the stock. When the curry is brought to the boil, tip in the slow cooker and cook on Low for 6–8 hours.

To pressure cook: Prepare in the same way. Cook at High Pressure for 8 minutes. Reduce the pressure quickly under cold water. Remove the lid and boil rapidly for a few minutes to reduce the liquid.

Dry Beef Curry

Preparation time:
15 minutes plus marinating
Cooking time:
1 hour 40 minutes
Freezeable for:
3 months

This is great served with a whole selection of accompaniments, like chopped onion, sliced banana, halved cherry tomatoes, chopped cucumber and radishes, desiccated coconut and raisins, raita, mango chutney and lime pickle.

- Mix all the spices together with the water. Add the beef, mix well with your hands to coat completely. Cover and marinate in the fridge for at least 2 hours, if time. It can be cooked immediately, if necessary.

- Melt the butter in a large saucepan. Add the onion and garlic and fry, stirring, for 2 minutes.

- Add the beef and fry, stirring, for 3–4 minutes until browned all over.

- Add the stock, bay leaf and a little salt and pepper, stir, bring to the boil, reduce the heat as low as possible, cover with foil then a lid and simmer very gently for 2 hours until tender.

- Remove the lid and boil rapidly for 1–2 minutes until the liquid has almost evaporated. Stir in the garam masala, taste and re-season, if necessary. Discard the bay leaf.

- Serve hot with plain basmati rice and a mixed vegetable curry.

To slow cook: Prepare as above, place in the crock pot and pour 150ml boiling stock over. Cover with a sheet of damp baking parchment and press down on top of the meat. Cook on Low for 10 hours. It will be moister than cooking conventionally.

To pressure cook: Prepare as above but use only 250ml stock. Cook at High Pressure for 15–20 minutes. Reduce the pressure quicly under cold water. If necessary, boil rapidly in the open cooker to evaporate the liquid.

Ingredients:

1 tbsp ground cumin
2 tsp ground coriander
1 tsp ground turmeric
½ tsp chilli powder
½ tsp ground cinnamon
¼ tsp ground cloves
2 tbsp water
700g skirt beef or lean braising steak, cut in small chunks
50g butter or ghee
1 onion, chopped (or a large handful frozen chopped onion)
1 garlic clove, crushed (or ½ tsp garlic purée)
300ml beef stock
1 bay leaf
Salt and freshly ground black pepper
1 tsp garam masala

To serve
Plain Basmati Rice (page 128)
Mixed Vegetable Curry (page 109)

Preparation time:
20 minutes
Cooking time:
2 hours
Freezable for:
3 months

Serves 4 • British • ♪

Simple Beef, Carrot and Mushroom Curry

Ingredients:
2 tbsp sunflower oil
2 onions, chopped (or
    2 large handfuls of frozen,
    chopped onions)
2 large carrots, diced
1 garlic clove, crushed (or
    ½ tsp garlic purée)
700g lean braising steak, cut
    in small chunks
3 tbsp Madras curry powder
    or paste
1 tbsp plain flour
450ml beef stock
3 tbsp smooth mango
    chutney
100g baby button
    mushrooms
Salt and freshly ground black
    pepper
2 bay leaves

This is more like a curried beef casserole but it does taste really good, particularly with some baby potatoes, tossed in a little sunflower oil and cumin seeds and roasted in a roasting tin on the top shelf for an hour or so.

- Preheat the oven to 160°C/Gas 3.

- Heat the oil in a flameproof casserole. Add the beef to the pan and fry, stirring, until browned all over. Remove with a slotted spoon and set aside.

- Add the onions and carrots to the casserole and fry for 3–4 minutes until lightly golden. Stir in the curry powder or paste and fry for 30 seconds. Stir in the flour, then gradually blend in the stock. Bring to the boil, stirring. Add the chutney.

- Return the beef to the casserole and add the mushrooms. Season to taste and tuck in the bay leaves. Cover and cook in the oven for at least 2 hours or until the beef is meltingly tender and bathed in a rich sauce.

- Discard the bay leaves, taste and re-season, if necessary.

To slow cook: Prepare as above but use only 300ml stock. Slow cook on Low for 8–10 hours.

To pressure cook: Prepare as above but use only 300ml stock. Pressure cook at High pressure for 15–20 minutes. Reduce pressure quickly under cold water.

Serves 4 • Asian • ♪♪

Curried Beef and Noodle Stew with Vegetables

Preparation time:
20 minutes
Cooking time:
2 hours
Freezeable for:
3 months without the noodles

Ideally use daikon – winter radish – for this Vietnamese-style recipe but 2 large turnips will do instead if you can't find one. You can substitute a large potato for the sweet potato and it tastes good with pork instead of beef for a change.

- Put everything except the noodles in a large saucepan. Bring to the boil, reduce the heat, part-cover and simmer very gently for 2 hours until the beef is meltingly tender.

- Meanwhile cook the rice noodles according to the packet directions. Drain.

- Remove the cinnamon stick, star anise and the bay leaf from the stew. Taste and re-season, if necessary.

- Spoon the noodles into large open bowls. Spoon the beef and vegetable stew over. Garnish with plenty of chopped fresh coriander and serve with hot chilli sauce to drizzle over, if liked.

To slow cook: Put everything except the stock and noodles in the slow cooker. Add 600ml boiling light beef stock. Slow cook on Low for 8–10 hours.

To pressure cook: Reduce the stock to 600ml. Put everything except the noodles in the pressure cooker. Cut the vegetables in slightly larger chunks. Cook at High Pressure for 20 minutes. Reduce the pressure quickly under cold water.

Ingredients:
1 bunch of spring onions, cut in short lengths
1 small sweet potato, cut into chunks
2 large carrots, cut into chunks
½ daikon, cut into chunks
500g thick slice of lean braising steak, cut in thin strips across the grain
2 garlic cloves, crushed (or 1 tsp garlic purée)
2 tsp grated fresh root ginger (or ginger purée)
2 fat red chillies, deseeded and cut in long, thin strips
1 tbsp Madras curry powder or paste
1 long piece of cinnamon stick
2 star anise
1 bay leaf
1 tsp soft light brown sugar
2 tbsp tomato purée
1 tbsp Thai fish sauce
Salt and freshly ground black pepper
750ml light beef stock
200g rice noodles

To garnish
Handful of chopped fresh coriander

To serve
Hot chilli sauce (optional)

Preparation time:
20 minutes

Cooking time:
30 minutes

Freezable for:
3 months, without the final
vegetables

Serves 4 • Asian • 🌶🌶

Rich Beef and Coconut Curry

This is a version of a Malaysian dish, called *rendang daging*, which I've made using small steaks, gently simmered in spices and coconut to make a dryish curry. To toast the coconut, simply dry-fry it in a non-stick frying pan, stirring until golden, then tip out into a dish immediately.

Ingredients:
4 tbsp sunflower oil
4 frying steaks (about 500g in all)
1 small onion, grated
1 large garlic clove, crushed (or 1 tsp garlic purée)
2 tsp grated of fresh root ginger (or ginger purée)
2 tsp crushed dried chillies, plus extra to garnish
¼ tsp ground cloves
400ml hot water
2 tsp finely chopped lemongrass (or lemongrass purée)
2 tsp tamarind paste
2 star anise
50g creamed coconut
1 tbsp soft light brown sugar
Salt
4 tbsp desiccated coconut, toasted
4 carrots, cut in matchsticks
2 pak choi, cut in chunky pieces
1 tsp Thai fish sauce

To serve
Perfect Thai Jasmine Rice (page 129)
Caribbean Roti Breads (page 135)

- Heat 1 tbsp of the oil in a large, shallow pan. Brown the steaks quickly on both sides. Remove from the pan and set aside.

- Mix the onion, garlic, ginger, chilli and cloves together with 1 tbsp of the water to a paste. Heat a further 2 tbsp of the oil in the pan and add the paste. Fry, stirring, until fragrant. Add the lemongrass, tamarind and star anise and cook, stirring for 30 seconds.

- Add the remaining water, the coconut and the sugar. Stir well, then add salt, to taste.

- Stir in the toasted coconut then return the beef to the pan, bring to the boil, reduce the heat, cover and simmer gently for 30 minutes until the beef is tender. If necessary, remove the lid and simmer a few minutes more to reduce the liquid to a thick, rich, almost dryish sauce.

- Meanwhile steam or boil the carrots until almost tender, about 5 minutes. Drain, if necessary.

- Heat the remaining oil in a frying pan or wok. Add the pak choi and stir-fry for 1 minute until wilting. Add the carrots and toss for 1 minute. Toss in the fish sauce.

- Put the steaks on plates and top with the vegetables. Sprinkle with a few chilli flakes. Serve with Jasmine rice or roti breads.

Serves 4 • Caribbean • 🌶🌶

Curried Beef with Olives, Raisins and Fried Eggs

Preparation time:
15 minutes
Cooking time:
1¾ hours
Freezeable for:
3 months, without the eggs

This is based on a Cuban speciality called picadillo. I first ate it in Havana but have adapted it to be more fragrant than fiery hot! The Cubans add a teaspoon of achiote to colour it, so do add if you like it. Use the liquid from the drained beef as stock for soup.

- Put the beef in a saucepan. Just cover with water and add ½ tsp salt. Bring to the boil, skim the surface, reduce the heat, cover and simmer very gently for 1½ hours until really tender. Drain, reserving the stock, then chop the meat.

- Heat the oil in a large frying pan. Add the onion and fry, stirring, for 3 minutes until softening and lightly golden.

- Add the garlic and peppers and fry for a further 2–3 minutes until the peppers are softening.

- Add the remaining ingredients except the eggs and coriander. Stir in 120ml of the reserved beef stock. Bring to the boil, reduce the heat and simmer gently, stirring occasionally, for 10 minutes or until thick and pulpy and the peppers are tender.

- Add the beef and moisten with a little more of the reserved stock, if necessary. Season to taste and heat through.

- Fry the eggs in a little oil until cooked to your liking.

- Spoon the beef mixture into shallow bowls, top with the eggs and a sprinkling of coriander. Serve with lime wedges, roti and salad.

To slow cook: Put the beef in the slow cooker, just-cover with boiling water. Add the the salt and cook on Low for 8–10 hours.

To pressure cook: Put the beef in the pressure cooker with just enough water to cover. Add the salt. Cook on High Pressure for 20 minutes. Reduce the pressure quickly under cold water.

Ingredients:
500g lean braising steak, cut into large chunks
Salt and freshly ground black pepper
2 tbsp sunflower oil, plus extra for frying
1 large onion, chopped (or 2 large handfuls of frozen chopped onion)
1 large garlic clove, crushed (or 1 tsp garlic purée)
1 large green pepper, deseeded and roughly chopped
1 large yellow pepper, deseeded and roughly chopped
2 fat red chillies, deseeded and finely chopped
2 tsp crushed dried chillies
½ tsp ground turmeric
1 tsp ground cumin
¼ tsp ground cloves
400g can of chopped tomatoes
2 tbsp tomato purée
1 tsp caster sugar
50g stuffed green olives, sliced
Handful of raisins
2 tsp red wine vinegar
4 eggs
1 tbsp chopped fresh coriander

To serve
Lime wedges
Caribbean Roti Breads (page 135)
Green salad

Preparation time:
15 minutes
Cooking time:
2 hours
Freezable for:
3 months

Serves 4 • Asian • ♪

Braised Curried Beef and Vegetables

Ingredients:
2 tsp ground coriander
1 tsp ground cumin
½ tsp crushed dried chillies
½ tsp ground cinnamon
2 cardamom pods, split,
    seeds extracted
¼ tsp ground turmeric
2 tsp finely chopped
    lemongrass (or lemongrass
    purée)
700g braising steak, cut in
    chunks
2 large garlic cloves, crushed
    (or 2 tsp garlic purée)
2 tsp grated fresh root
    ginger or ginger purée
8 baby potatoes, halved
16 baby carrots, scrubbed
6 baby sweetcorn, halved
2 tbsp soy sauce
2 tsp soft light brown sugar
400ml can of coconut milk
400g can of tomatoes
2 tbsp chopped fresh horapa
    (Thai basil) or ordinary
    basil (optional)

To serve
Crusty bread or Caribbean
    Roti Bread (page 135)
Small green salad

A very fragrant with a mix with Asian influences, this curry takes very little preparation so is great to shove in the oven then go off and do something else whilst it cooks (or use the slow- or pressure-cooking method to suit your lifestyle).

- Preheat the oven to 180°C/Gas 4.

- Mix everything together in a flameproof casserole. Bring to the boil, stirring, cover and place in the oven. Cook for 2 hours until really tender.

- Taste and re-season if necessary.

- Spoon into bowls, sprinkle with the horapa or basil and serve with crusty bread or roti and a small green salad.

To slow cook: Mix the meat and spices in the crock pot. Bring the tomatoes and coconut milk to the boil in a pan, pour over, stir, cover and cook on Low for 8–10 hours.

To pressure cook: Cook at High Pressure for 20 minutes. Release pressure quickly under cold water. If necessary, boil rapidly in the open cooker to thicken the liquid.

Curried Steak Kebabs with Chickpea Couscous

Preparation time:
25 minutes
Cooking time:
11–17 minutes
Not suitable for freezing

These steak kebabs are great for a quick dinner – they only need marinating for half an hour, so get that done first whilst preparing the couscous and then they'll be ready to cook. Make sure you serve with a crisp green salad.

- Mix 1 tbsp of the oil with the vinegar, half the garlic, all the spices and a little salt and pepper in a shallow container. Add the steak, toss well, cover and chill in the fridge for at least 30 minutes (it can be all day, or overnight, if necessary). If you are using wooden skewers, you can soak them at the same time.

- When nearly ready to grill the meat, put the couscous in a bowl. Add the boiling stock, stir and leave to stand for 5 minutes.

- Heat the remaining oil in a frying pan. Add the cumin and sesame seeds and fry for 30 minutes, stirring, until the cumin is fragrant and the sesame seeds are turning golden. Remove from the heat and add the lemon juice. Stir into the couscous with the chickpeas and chilli. Put the bowl over a pan of simmering water, cover and steam to heat through whilst the meat cooks.

- Preheat the grill. Thread the steak on 8 metal or the soaked wooden skewers and grill for 6–12 minutes, depending on how you like your steak, turning once or twice.

- Make the dressing. Mix all the ingredients together with the remaining garlic. Season to taste.

- When the meat is cooked, fluff up the couscous and pile on plates. Top with the kebabs and spoon some of the dressing to one side.

Ingredients:
- 3 tbsp sunflower oil
- 1 tbsp balsamic vinegar
- 1 large garlic clove crushed (or 1 tsp garlic purée)
- 2 tsp grated fresh root ginger (or ginger purée)
- 1 tsp ground coriander
- ½ tsp chilli powder
- ½ tsp ground turmeric
- ½ tsp ground cumin
- Salt and freshly ground black pepper
- 600g lean rump or fillet steak, cubed

For the couscous
- 250g couscous
- 400ml boiling beef or vegetable stock
- 2 tsp cumin seeds
- 2 tsp sesame seeds
- 1 tbsp lemon juice
- 400g can of chickpeas (drained)
- 1 fat red chilli, deseeded, if liked, and finely chopped

For the dressing
- 150ml thick plain yoghurt
- 2 tsp dried mint
- 3 tbsp chopped fresh or frozen coriander
- 1 small avocado, peeled, stoned and finely diced

Lamb Curries

Lamb is a sweet meat but can be fatty so trim it well before cooking, if necessary. Older lamb or mutton has the best flavour for currying – the young spring lamb is too delicate. Lamb is incredibly versatile, with shanks, chops and whole joints to take the curry treatment as well as minced and diced meat. Because lamb is so popular in Middle Eastern cuisine, I've taken some of their influences for a few of the dishes as well as some from further East from Asia and India and West to the Caribbean. There is also a simple curried lamb pasty recipe to use up the remains of the Sunday roast, or you can use it in a biryani (page 51). Goat is an up-and-coming meat, now available in the UK. It is low in fat and great in taste and can be substituted for lamb in any of these dishes. Give it a go – you'll find it online if your local butcher doesn't stock it – I am sure you will be very pleasantly surprised!

Preparation time:
15 minutes
Cooking time:
45 minutes
Freezable for:
3 months, without the celeriac

Serves 4 • Indian • ♪♪

Lamb Rogan Josh

Ingredients:
2 tbsp sunflower oil
3 tsp cumin seeds
1 tsp coriander seeds
1 tsp black mustard seeds
2 cardamom pods, split,
    seeds extracted
1 tbsp sweet paprika
½ tsp ground cinnamon
½ tsp chilli powder
¼ tsp ground fenugreek
¼ tsp ground cloves
1 small onion, roughly
    chopped
2 garlic cloves, crushed (or
    1 tsp garlic purée)
2 tbsp water
600g lean leg or neck fillet
    of lamb, diced (not too
    big)
200ml plain yoghurt
200ml lamb or chicken stock
½ tsp caster sugar
2 tbsp tomato purée
Salt
1 small celeriac, peeled and
    cut in small chunks
A knob of butter
2 tsp fennel or caraway seeds
Salt

To serve
Chapattis (page 133)
Mixed Salad with Cumin and
    Onion Seed Dressing
    (page 141)

This medium saucy curry is delicious with the chapattis or naan to mop up all the sauce. For a change from rice, I've crushed some celeriac with some toasted spice seeds to act as a base.

- Heat half the oil in a saucepan and fry 1 tsp of the cumin seeds (reserve the rest for the celeriac), all the coriander and mustard seeds for 30 seconds until fragrant. Tip into a mortar or small food processor. Add the remaining spices, the onion, garlic and water and pound or grind to a paste.

- Heat the remaining oil in the saucepan. Add the lamb and brown on all sides. Add the spice mix and fry for 30 seconds, stirring.

- Add the yoghurt, stock, sugar and tomato purée. Stir well. Bring to the boil (it will curdle), reduce the heat, cover and simmer gently for about 45 minutes or until the lamb is really tender.

- Meanwhile, boil the celeriac in salted water for about 10 minutes until tender. Drain.

- Heat the remaining oil and the butter in the saucepan. Add the remaining fennel seeds and the cumin seeds. Fry for 30 seconds, stirring, until fragrant. Turn down the heat as low as possible. Add the celeriac, coarsely crush with a potato masher, stir and season.

- Spoon the crushed celeriac into bowls. Spoon the lamb curry over. Serve with chapattis and a mixed salad.

To slow cook: Reduce yoghurt and stock to 150ml each. Bring to the boil, tip into the crock pot and cook on Low for 6–8 hours.

To pressure cook: Reduce the yoghurt and stock to 150ml each. Cook at High Pressure for 10 minutes, Reduce the pressure quickly under cold water, then boil rapidly in the open pan to thicken.

• Lamb Curries

Serves 4 • Indian • ♪

Lamb Biryani

Preparation time:
15 minutes
Cooking time:
80 minutes

You can use different meats for a biryani, using a similar method. Or you can use leftover cooked meat, omitting the stock and cooking for 20 minutes.

- Heat the oil in a large saucepan. Add the onions and fry for about 5 minutes, stirring until soft and golden. Remove half and reserve for garnish. Add the lamb to the remaining onion and brown on all sides. Add all the spices, the bay leaf and a little salt and pepper. Cook, stirring, for 1 minute.

- Stir in the yoghurt and the stock. Bring to the boil, then reduce the heat, cover and simmer gently for 1 hour.

- Remove the lid and continue to simmer, stirring occasionally, for a further 5–10 minutes until the liquid has evaporated and the meat is tender and bathed in a rich sauce.

- Meanwhile, cook the rice in boiling, salted water for 10 minutes, adding the peas half way through cooking. Drain and return to the pan. Add the lamb to the rice, stirring well. Taste and re-season, if necessary.

- Meanwhile, reheat the extra fried onions and stir in the dried fruit and nuts.

- Spoon the biryani on to plates, garnish with the fruit and nut mixture, and serve with popadoms, a side salad and cucumber raita.

2 tbsp sunflower oil
2 large onions, sliced
500g diced lean lamb
1 tsp grated fresh root
ginger (or ginger purée)
1 garlic clove, crushed (or
½ tsp garlic purée)
¼ tsp chilli powder
1 tsp ground cumin
1 tsp ground coriander
1 tsp ground turmeric
1 bay leaf
Salt and freshly ground
black pepper
250ml plain yoghurt
250ml lamb or chicken
stock
350g basmati rice
100g frozen peas

To garnish
2 tbsp raisins or currants
2 tbsp toasted flaked
coconut or almonds

To serve
Popadoms, Cucumber Raita
(page 137) and a mixed
salad

Preparation time:
20 minutes plus marinating
Cooking time:
1½ hours
Freezeable for:
3 months

Ingredients:

2 garlic cloves, crushed (or
  1 tsp garlic purée)
2 tsp grated fresh root
  ginger (or ginger purée)
1 tsp ground turmeric
1 tsp ground cinnamon
2 cardamom pods, split,
  seeds extracted
¼ tsp chilli powder
2 tbsp water
700g lean lamb, diced
2 tbsp sunflower oil
25g butter or ghee
2 onions, finely chopped (or
  2 large handfuls of
  chopped frozen onion)
450ml chicken stock
5 tbsp desiccated coconut
1 tsp caster sugar
Salt and freshly ground black
  pepper
150ml crème fraîche
1 tbsp chopped fresh
  coriander or mint, plus
  extra to garnish

To serve
Simple Yellow Pilau Rice
  (page 130)
Avocado Sambal (page 144)

Serves 4 • Indian • ♪

Creamy Coconut Lamb Curry

A mild, creamy korma curry, this can be cooked in the oven instead of on the hob if you prefer. Simply cook at 180°C/Gas 4 for the same amount of time. You can use 3 tbsp Korma paste and omit the coconut instead of using the home-made spice paste.

- Mix the garlic and spices together with the water to form a paste in a large plastic container with a lid. Add the meat and mix well with your hands. Cover and leave to marinate in the fridge for several hours, all day, or overnight if more convenient.

- Heat the oil and butter in a heavy-based saucepan. Add the onions and fry, stirring for 5 minutes until golden. Add the meat and fry, stirring until browned all over.

- Stir in the stock, coconut, sugar and some salt and pepper. Bring to the boil, stir well, cover, reduce the heat and simmer very gently for 1½ hours or until the lamb is tender and bathed in sauce.

- Stir in the crème fraîche, taste and re-season if necessary.

- Spoon over pilau rice, garnish with chopped coriander or mint, and serve with an avocado sambal.

To slow cook: Reduce the stock to 250ml. Tip into the crock pot and cook on Low for 8–10 hours.

To pressure cook: Reduce the stock to 250ml. Cook at High Pressure for 15–20 minutes. Reduce the pressure quickly under cold water. Boil rapidly in open pan, if necessary, to thicken sauce.

Quick Lamb Madras

Preparation time:
15 minutes
Cooking time:
20 minutes
Freezable for:
3 months

This is an easy-to-make curry that doesn't take long to cook because it uses tender lamb neck fillets. You could use pork fillet instead. To make it milder, omit the chilli powder and just use the curry powder or paste.

- Mix the lemon or lime juice, garlic, garam masala and salt together. Add the lamb and turn over in the mixture to coat completely.

- Heat the oil in a large saucepan. Add the onion and fry, stirring, for 3–4 minutes until lightly golden.

- Stir in the curry powder or paste and cook, stirring, for 30 seconds.

- Add the lamb and fry, stirring, until lightly browned all over.

- Add the tomatoes, coconut milk, tomato purée and mango chutney. Bring to the boil, reduce the heat and simmer gently for 30 minutes, stirring occasionally, until the sauce is rich and thick and the lamb is tender. Stir in the coriander. Taste and re-season if necessary.

- Serve with mango chutney, chapattis and a mixed salad.

Ingredients:
1 tbsp lemon or lime juice
1 garlic clove, crushed (or ½ tsp garlic purée)
2 tsp garam masala
½ tsp salt
600g lamb neck fillet, trimmed and diced
2 tbsp sunflower oil
1 large onion chopped (or 2 large handfuls of frozen chopped onion)
4 tbsp Madras curry powder or paste
½ tsp chilli powder
4 tomatoes, chopped
400ml can of coconut milk
2 tbsp tomato purée
2 tbsp mango chutney
2 tbsp chopped fresh or frozen coriander

To serve
Extra mango chutney
Chapattis (page 133) or use bought
Mixed Salad with Cumin and Onion Seed Dressing (page 141)

Preparation time:
20 minutes
Cooking time:
20–25 minutes
Freezeable for:
3 months

Serves 4 • Indian • ♪♪

Lamb, Spinach and Sultana Curry

Ingredients:
2 tbsp sunflower oil
1 large onion, chopped (or
   2 handfuls of frozen
   chopped onion)
1 tsp cumin seeds
600g lamb neck fillets, cut
   into chunky slices
2 garlic cloves, crushed (or
   1 tsp garlic purée)
2 tsp grated fresh root
   ginger (or ginger purée)
1 tbsp sweet paprika
2 fat green chillies,
   deseeded, if liked, and
   finely chopped
½ tsp ground cinnamon
2 bay leaves
1 tsp salt
1 tsp soft light brown sugar
250ml lamb or chicken stock
200g fresh baby leaf spinach
3 tbsp sultanas
2 tsp garam masala

To serve
Plain Basmati Rice (page
   128)
Carrot and Beetroot Salad
   with Mustard Yoghurt
   Dressing (page 140)

This is my latest version of *palak gosht* – a Northern Indian dish with a good, rich flavour. It doesn't take long to cook so is good for a midweek supper. You can use skinless chicken breast, diced instead of the lamb if you prefer, but cook for 10 minutes.

- Heat the oil in a saucepan. Add the onion, and fry, stirring, for 2 minutes.

- Add the cumin and fry for 30 seconds until fragrant. Add the lamb and fry, stirring, for 2 minutes.

- Stir in the remaining ingredients except the spinach, sultanas and garam masala. Bring to the boil, reduce the heat, part-cover and simmer gently for 15 minutes.

- Wash the spinach thoroughly and shake off the excess moisture. Roughly chop and add to the pan with the sultanas. Cook, stirring, for 5 minutes until the spinach is wilted. If necessary, boil rapidly to reduce the liquid.

- Stir in the garam masala, taste and re-season if necessary.

- Serve with plain basmati rice and the carrot and beetroot salad.

Serves 4 • Indian • ♪♪

Indian-style Slow-roast Lamb Shanks

Preparation time:
25 minutes
Cooking time:
3 hours
Freezable for:
3 months

Lamb shanks need long, slow cooking so are perfect for slow cooking in the oven or slow cooker. I don't recommend pressure cooking them as the meat tends to shrink too quickly and, literally falls off the bones, which is tenderising too far!

- Put the lamb shanks in a large casserole dish, to hold them in a single layer, spread the spice mixture all over the lamb.

- Mix the garlic with the ginger, almonds, chillies, paprika, salt, sugar, yoghurt and tomato purée.

- Preheat the oven to 150°C/Gas 2.

- Heat the oil in a frying pan, add shallots and fry for 1–2 minutes, stirring, until lightly golden.

- Add all the seeds, the cinnamon stick, curry leaves and a good grinding of pepper and cook until the seeds begin to pop. Spoon this mixture over the lamb.

- Add the water to the casserole, cover and cook in the oven for 3 hours or until meltingly tender.

- Lift the meat out of the casserole. Spoon off all the fat. Discard the cinnamon stick and curry leaves. Stir the sauce, adding a little more boiling water if the sauce is too thick. Taste and re-season, if necessary.

- Serve the lamb on a bed of rice with the sauce spooned over and a green salad.

To slow cook: Prepare as above but put it all in the crock pot, and add only 250ml boiling water. Cover and cook on Low for 10 hours.

Ingredients:
4 lamb shanks
2 garlic cloves, crushed (or 1 tsp garlic purée)
1 tsp grated fresh root ginger (or ginger purée)
25g ground almonds
2 fat red chillies, deseeded, if liked, and finely chopped
1 tbsp sweet paprika
1 tsp salt
1 tsp soft light brown sugar
120ml plain yoghurt
2 tbsp tomato purée
6 tbsp sunflower oil
2 shallots, finely chopped (or 2 tbsp frozen chopped shallot)
2 tsp cumin seeds
2 tsp black onion seeds
4 cardamom pods, split and seeds extracted
1 large piece of cinnamon stick
4 curry leaves
Freshly ground black pepper
450ml boiling water

To serve
Plain Basmati Rice (page 128)
Spiced Green Salad (page 142)

Lamb, Fresh Date and Curry-spiced Tagine

Preparation time:
25 minutes
Cooking time:
1½ hours
Freezeable for:
3 months, without the courgettes

Ingredients:
1 tbsp sunflower oil
A knob of butter
1 bunch of spring onions, chopped
2 garlic cloves crushed (or 1 tsp garlic purée)
1 tsp grated fresh root ginger (or ginger purée)
2 tsp ground cinnamon
1 star anise
1 tsp ground cumin
½ tsp chilli powder
1 tbsp ground paprika
1 tsp ground turmeric
1 tsp asafoetida (optional)
2 curry leaves or 1 bay leaf
700g lean lamb, diced
400g can of chopped tomatoes
200ml lamb or chicken stock
1 tsp dried oregano
1 green pepper, diced
1 fat green chilli, deseeded, if liked, and thinly sliced
8 fresh dates, stoned and quartered
Salt and freshly ground black pepper
2 tbsp tomato purée
1 tsp clear honey
4 courgettes, cut into fingers

To serve
Couscous

A tagine is a conical-shaped earthenware casserole that allows the meat to steam gently inside. Dishes cooked in a tagine are often quite mild but this one is really hot and spicy. You can use an ordinary casserole dish instead or simmer very gently on the hob for the same length of time.

- Preheat the oven to 180°C/Gas 4.

- Heat the oil and butter in a flameproof casserole. Add the spring onions and fry for 2 minutes, stirring.

- Add all the spices and the curry leaves or bay leaf and fry for 30 seconds. Add the lamb and fry, stirring for 3–4 minutes until browned all over.

- Stir in the remaining ingredients except the tomato purée, honey and courgettes. Bring to the boil, cover and cook in the oven for 1½ hours until really tender.

- When almost ready, steam the courgettes for 5 minutes, then drain.

- Remove the tagine from the oven, stir in the tomato purée and honey and simmer 2 minutes. Taste and re-season if necessary.

- Stir in the steamed courgettes and serve with couscous.

To slow cook: Prepare as above but use only 100ml stock. Bring to the boil, then tip into the crock pot. Cook on Low for 8–10 hours.

To pressure cook: Prepare as above but use only 150ml stock. Cook at High Pressure for 10 minutes. Reduce the pressure quickly under cold water. Boil rapidly in the open cooker to reduce the liquid if necessary.

• Lamb Curries

Lamb Curry with Whole Spices

Preparation time:
20 minutes
Cooking time:
2 hours
Freezable for:
3 months, without the garnish

This is my fairly hot version of a dopiaza curry but there are numerous recipes, some very mild, some extremely hot. It is always made with some whole spices, which are left in the dish when serving to be fished out by the diner.

- Mix the ground spices with the grated onion, garlic and chopped chilli, then stir in 3 tbsp of the water to form a paste.

- Preheat the oven to 180°C/Gas 4.

- Heat half the oil in a flameproof casserole. Add the lamb and brown on all sides. Add the spice paste and curry leaves and fry for 1 minute, stirring. Add the remaining water, tomato purée, yoghurt, spices and some salt. Bring to the boil, stirring.

- Cover and cook in the oven for 2 hours until the lamb is tender and bathed in a rich sauce. Or simmer on the hob over a very low heat, checking frequently and adding more water, if necessary.

- Meanwhile heat the remaining oil in a large frying pan or wok and fry the onions, stirring, for about 4 minutes until soft and golden.

- Add the carrots and fry for a further 2 minutes, stirring until softened. Stir in the garam masala.

- When the curry is cooked, spoon off the excess oil, taste and add more salt, if necessary. Garnish with the fried onion and carrot and serve with naan breads and curried green beans.

To slow cook: Prepare as above but use only 150ml water. Cook on High for 5 hours or Low for 10 hours.

To pressure cook: Prepare as above but use only 150ml water. Cook at High Pressure for 10–15 minutes. Reduce the pressure quickly under cold water.

Ingredients:
1 tsp ground cumin
1 tsp ground coriander
½ tsp ground cloves
¼ tsp coarse ground black pepper
½ tsp chilli powder
1 small onion, grated
3 garlic cloves, crushed (or 1½ tsp garlic purée)
2 thin green chillies, deseeded, if liked, and finely chopped
250ml water
4 tbsp sunflower oil
700g lean lamb, diced
2 curry leaves
2 tbsp tomato purée
120ml plain yoghurt
1 piece of cinnamon stick
1 star anise
6 cardamom pods, split
Salt
3 large onions, halved and thinly sliced
2 large carrots, pared with a potato peeler
1 tsp garam masala

To serve
Garlic and Coriander Naans (page 132) or use bought
Curried Green Beans with Tomato (page 115) or Spiced Green Salad (page 142)

Preparation time:
15 minutes
Cooking time:
15 minutes
Not suitable for freezing

Serves 4 • British • ♪

Creamy Curried Kidneys with Mushrooms

Ingredients:
3 tbsp sunflower oil
8 lambs' kidneys, halved, cored and cut in chunks
1 small onion, grated
2 garlic cloves, crushed (or 1 tsp garlic purée)
1 tbsp Madras curry powder or paste
¼ tsp chilli powder
½ tsp English mustard
2 tbsp tomato purée
1 tbsp smooth mango chutney
4 tbsp water
12 button mushrooms, halved
Salt and freshly ground black pepper
5 tbsp double cream
2 tbsp chopped fresh parsley

To serve
Plain Basmati Rice (page 128)
Crisp green salad

This is a delicious version of devilled kidneys with a little kick of chilli but also a smooth, creamy sauce with a hint of coconut. You could use pork kidneys, cut in chunks in place of lamb's but they won't be quite as tender.

- Heat half the oil in a saucepan and fry the kidneys stirring for 2 minutes only. Remove with a slotted spoon and set aside.

- Heat the remaining oil in the pan and gently fry the onion for 5 minutes, stirring, until soft and only lightly golden.

- Stir in the garlic, curry powder and chilli powder and stir for 30 seconds. Add the mustard, tomato purée, mango chutney and water and stir well. Return the kidneys to the pan and stir in the mushrooms. Season with salt and pepper, cover and simmer very gently for 6–8 minutes until the kidneys are tender and everything is bathed in a rich sauce.

- Stir in the cream and re-season to taste. Spoon the kidneys over boiled rice, sprinkle with chopped fresh parsley and serve with a crisp green salad.

• Lamb Curries

Serves 4 • African • 🍌

Bobotie with potatoes and Butternut Squash

Preparation
25 minutes
Cooking time:
1 hour
Not suitable for freezing

This originated in South Africa and is like a curried shepherd's pie with a smooth custard topping. I've added some diced butternut squash and mango chutney for added sweetness and a layer of sliced potatoes under the custard for extra texture.

- Soak the bread in the milk.

- Heat the oil in a large saucepan, add the onions, lamb and butternut squash and fry, stirring, for about 5 minutes until the meat is no longer pink and all the grains are separate and the squash is nearly tender.

- Stir in the curry powder or paste and cook for 1 minute, stirring. Remove from the heat.

- Preheat the oven to 160°C/Gas 3.

- Beat the soaked bread and the milk into the meat with the lemon juice, mango chutney, raisins, almonds, basil and some salt and pepper. Place in a deep 1.5 litre ovenproof dish, set on a baking sheet.

- Boil the potatoes in lightly salted water for 3–4 minutes until just tender. Drain well and arrange overlapping over the meat mixture.

- Beat the eggs with the crème fraîche, nutmeg and a little salt and pepper. Pour over the top of the potatoes. Bake in the oven for about 1 hour until the topping is set and turning lightly golden.

- Sprinkle with the coconut and serve with rice and a crisp green salad.

Ingredients:
1 thick slice of wholemeal bread
250ml milk
2 tbsp sunflower oil
2 onions, chopped (or 2 large handfuls of frozen chopped onion)
600g minced lamb
½ butternut squash, halved, deseeded and diced
2 tbsp Madras curry powder or paste
1 tbsp lemon juice
1 tbsp smooth mango chutney
4 tbsp raisins
4 tbsp flaked almonds
½ tsp dried basil
Salt and freshly ground black pepper
2 potatoes, scrubbed and thinly sliced
2 eggs, beaten
200ml crème fraîche
A pinch of grated nutmeg
1 tbsp desiccated coconut

To serve
Plain Basmati Rice (page 128),
Crisp green salad

Caribbean Curried Lamb

Ingredients:
Large knob of butter
1 tbsp sunflower oil
8 lamb chops
1 large onion, chopped (or
   2 large handfuls of frozen
   chopped onion)
2 fat red chillies, deseeded,
   if liked, and chopped
2 tsp crushed dried chillies
2 tbsp Madras curry powder
   or paste
¼ tsp ground allspice
2 garlic cloves, finely
   chopped (or 1 tsp garlic
   purée)
1 beefsteak tomato, seeded
   and chopped
400ml can of coconut milk
300ml lamb or chicken stock
1 tsp dried oregano
Salt to taste
Juice of ½ lime

To garnish
Lime wedges and a small
   handful of torn fresh
   coriander

To serve
Roti Breads (page 135) or
   Yellow Rice (page 130)
Avocado Sambal (page 144)

Freezable for:
3 months

When I first tried this Jamaican-influenced dish it was made with goat and I thoroughly recommend it if you can buy some. Using meat on the bone gives the best flavour but you can use 600g diced boned lamb if you prefer. The long simmering gives a wonderful, rich sauce.

- Heat the butter and oil in a pan, add the chops and brown on both sides. Remove with a slotted spoon and set aside.
- Add the onion to the pan and fry, stirring, for 2 minutes.
- Stir in the chilli, curry powder or paste and allspice and fry for a further 30 seconds. Stir in all the remaining ingredients, bring to the boil and return the lamb to the pan.
- Reduce the heat, part-cover and simmer gently for 1½–2 hours until meltingly tender. Taste and re-season if necessary.
- Garnish with lime wedges and plenty of torn coriander serve with roti breads or yellow rice and the avocado sambal.

To slow cook: Put the browned lamb in the crock pot. Use only 100ml stock. Add the boiling sauce to the lamb, cover and cook on Low for 6–8 hours. If necessary, pour the sauce into a small saucepan and boil rapidly to reduce.

To pressure cook: Prepare as above, add only 100ml stock. Cook at High Pressure for 15–20 minutes. Reduce the pressure quickly under cold water. If necessary, boil in the open cooker for a few minutes to reduce the sauce.

Serves 4 • British • ♪

Preparation time:
30 minutes
Cooking time:
40 minutes
Not suitable for freezing

Curried Lamb Pasties with Curried Baked Beans

A delicious way to use up a small amount of roast lamb from the Sunday joint, you could use beef, pork or chicken instead. Just make sure you have plenty of mango chutney and raita to serve alongside and a crisp green salad.

- Preheat the oven to 200°C/Gas 6 and lightly grease a baking sheet.

- Mix all the vegetables in a large bowl with the lamb, curry powder, tomato purée and some salt and pepper.

- Roll out the pastry and cut into 4 x 20cm rounds, using a small plate as a guide. Divide the filling amongst the centres of the pastry rounds. Brush the edges with beaten egg.

- Doing each pasty in turn, add 2–3 tbsp water to the filling, draw up the edges of the pastry over the filling, meeting in the middle over the top. Pinch together then crimp between finger and thumb to form an attractive rippled edge down the centre of each pasty.

- Carefully transfer to the prepared baking sheet. Brush with beaten egg to glaze. Bake in the oven for 20 minutes until browned then cover loosely with foil and bake for a further 20 minutes until the filling is cooked through and the pastry is crisp and richly golden.

- Meanwhile, make the curried beans. Empty the contents of the baked beans into a small saucepan. Stir in the sultanas, curry powder and coriander. Heat gently, stirring until blended. Bring to the boil, reduce the heat and simmer gently for 1 minute. Serve the pasties hot with the curried baked beans and a crisp green salad.

Ingredients:
1 potato, peeled and finely diced
1 carrot, finely diced
1 celery stick, finely chopped
1 onion, finely chopped (or 1 large handful of frozen chopped onion)
200g cooked roast lamb, very finely chopped
2 tbsp Madras curry powder or paste
1 tbsp tomato purée
Salt and freshly ground black pepper
500g ready-made shortcrust pastry, thawed if frozen
Beaten egg, to glaze

For the curried beans:
400g can baked beans in tomato sauce
Handful of sultanas
2 tsp Madras curry powder or paste
1 tbsp chopped fresh or frozen coriander

To serve
Crisp green salad

Pork Curries

Pork, like beef, isn't as obvious a choice as lamb and chicken for the spice treatment (though many of those recipes can also be made with pork, as you'll see in the relevant chapters). However, I've created a whole selection of delicious speciality pork dishes for you to try. Using spices helps to offset the richness of pork and, because it has a robust flavour anyway, it can support deep flavour combinations that make for sensational eating! Here you'll find everything from my Goan-style pork curry, a more traditional curry and one of the hottest I can stand, to a wonderful Cajun-meets-Thai spiced pork steaks recipe. India also meets China most harmoniously with my delicious sticky mango curried ribs – a mouth-watering union indeed!

CHAPTER 10

Preparation time:
10 minutes
Cooking time:
1 hour 40 minutes
Freezable for:
2 months

Serves 4 • Indian • ♪

Mango Curried Ribs

Ingredients:
900g pork short spare ribs
2 tbsp red wine vinegar
3 tbsp smooth mango
   chutney
1 tbsp clear honey
2 tbsp dark soy sauce
1 tsp tamarind paste
2 tbsp Madras curry paste

To serve
Baked Mushroom Pilau Rice
   (page 131)
Spiced Green Salad (page
   142)

These succulently tender ribs have a lovely sticky coating from the mango chutney and honey, blended with Indian curry spices and a splash of soy – an awesome combination! I've served them with the mushroom pilau for a main meal but you could serve them as a starter for up to six.

• Place the ribs in a large pan and cover with water. Add half the vinegar. Bring to the boil, reduce the heat, cover and simmer gently for 1 hour. Alternatively, pressure Cook at High Pressure for 10 minutes then reduce the pressure quickly under cold water. Drain thoroughly and return to the saucepan.

• Preheat the oven to 180°C /Gas 4. Dampen a roasting tin and line completely with a sheet of non-stick baking parchment, making sure it comes up the sides of the tin (to prevent the glaze sticking to the tin).

• Mix together all the remaining ingredients. Pour over the ribs and toss to coat completely in the sauce.

• Arrange the ribs in the prepared tin in a single layer. Spoon over any remaining sauce. (Prepare the mushroom pilau now so it cooks at the same time.)

• Roast in the oven for about 40 minutes, turning once until meltingly tender and stickily glazed.

• Serve hot with the mushroom pilau and a green salad.

To slow cook: Mix the raw ribs in all the coating ingredients. Place in large slow cooker, lined with baking parchment, and cook on Low for 6–8 hours until meltingly tender, turning and rearranging once.

Serves 4 • Asian • ♪♪♪

Thai Chai Curry

Preparation time:
10 minutes
Cooking time:
40 minutes
Freezeable for:
3 months

This is a fusion dish where Thai food meets Chinese – hence the name! The flavours complement each other perfectly and work with a Thai rice or Chinese noodle accompaniment. Add more chillies if you like a hotter curry.

- Mix the bean sauce with the curry paste, chillies, onion, garlic, galangal, lemongrass, tamarind paste, fish sauce and sugar in a large saucepan. Add the pork and toss well to coat.

- Stir in the coconut milk and stock, bring to the boil, reduce the heat, cover and simmer very gently for 40 minutes until the pork is really tender.

- Spoon over jasmine rice or Chinese egg noodles and scatter the coriander over. Serve with a Thai-style green salad.

To slow cook: Prepare as above, bring to the boil, tip in the slow cooker and cook on Low for 6–8 hours.

To pressure cook: Prepare as above but cook at High Pressure for 10 minutes. Reduce the pressure quickly under cold water.

Ingredients:
4 tbsp black bean sauce
4 tbsp Thai red curry paste
2 thin red chillies, deseeded, if liked, and finely chopped
1 large onion, finely chopped (or 2 large handfuls of frozen chopped onion)
2 garlic cloves, crushed (or 1 tsp garlic purée)
1 tbsp grated galangal or fresh root ginger (or galangal or ginger purée)
1 tsp finely chopped lemongrass (or lemongrass purée)
2 tsp tamarind paste
1 tbsp Thai fish sauce
1 tbsp soft light brown sugar
600g pork stir-fry meat (or pork leg, cut in thin strips)
400ml can of coconut milk
120ml light chicken stock

To garnish
Handful of torn coriander leaves

To serve
Perfect Thai Jasmine Rice (page 129) or Chinese egg noodles
Thai-style Green Salad (page 139)

Preparation time:
10 minutes
Cooking time:
45 minutes
Freezable for:
3 months

Serves 4 • Asian • ♪♪

Burmese-style Pork Curry

Ingredients:
3 tbsp sunflower oil
500g pork stir-fry meat (or
  pork leg, cut in thin strips)
1 large onion, chopped (or
  2 large handfuls of frozen
  chopped onion)
1 large garlic clove, crushed
  (or 1 tsp garlic purée)
2 tsp grated galangal (or
  galangal purée)
1 tsp ground turmeric
1 tsp ground cumin
1 tsp ground coriander
2–3 thin red chillies,
  deseeded, if liked, and
  finely chopped
400ml can of coconut milk
120ml light chicken stock
2 tbsp soy sauce
2 tsp soft light brown sugar
50g roasted (preferably
  unsalted) peanuts or
  cashew nuts
2 spring onions, finely
  chopped

To serve
Perfect Thai Jasmine Rice
  (page 129)

This rich curry is based on those from the Myanmar region. The peanuts add an interesting texture. Use ginger instead of galangal if you prefer. For added crunch, serve it with small bowls of bean sprouts to throw in as you eat.

• Heat half the oil in a large saucepan or wok. Add the pork and stir-fry for 2–3 minutes until browned all over. Remove from the pan with a slotted spoon.

• Heat the remaining oil, add the onion to the pan and fry for 2 minutes, stirring, then stir in the garlic, and spices and fry for 30 seconds.

• Return the pork to the pan. Add the coconut milk, stock, soy sauce and sugar. Bring to the boil, reduce the heat, cover and simmer very gently for 40 minutes or until the pork is tender.

• Stir in the nuts and simmer gently for a further 5 minutes. Taste and add more soy sauce if necessary.

• Serve spooned over jasmine rice, garnished with chopped spring onion.

To slow cook: Prepare as above, bring to the boil then tip into the crock pot and cook on Low for 8 hours.

To pressure cook: Prepare as above but cook at High Pressure for 10 minutes. Reduce the pressure quickly under cold water.

Serves 4 • Indian • ♪♪♪

Goan-style Pork Curry

Preparation time:
20 minutes
Cooking time:
1–1½ hours
Freezeable for:
3 months

This is a very hot, sharp curry based on those from the Indian island of Goa, similar to a vindaloo. Even though it's pretty fiery, there is a huge amount of flavour coming through. Try drinking a lassi (page 146) with it to quash the fire.

- Toast the cumin and coriander seeds in a dry frying pan for 30 seconds, stirring, until fragrant. Tip into a mortar or small food processor. Add the onion, garlic, all the other spices and 2 tbsp of the water. Pound or grind to a paste.

- Heat the oil in a large saucepan. Add the pork and fry for 2–3 minutes, stirring and turning until browned all over.

- Add the spice paste and fry for a further 30 seconds, stirring. Add the remaining water, vinegar, sugar, salt and bay leaves. Bring to the boil, reduce the heat, part-cover and simmer gently for 1–1½ hours until the pork is really tender, adding a little more water, if becoming too dry. Discard the bay leaves.

- Serve with plain basmati rice and the carrot and beetroot salad.

To slow cook: Prepare as above but use 200ml water. Bring to the boil, tip into the crock pot and cook on Low for 8 hours.

To pressure cook: Prepare as above but use only 200ml water. Cook at High Pressure for 15 minutes. Cool quickly under cold water.

Ingredients:
2 tbsp sunflower oil
1 tbsp cumin seeds
2 tsp coriander seeds
1 large onion, roughly
    chopped (or 2 large
    handfuls of frozen chopped
    onion)
2 garlic cloves, crushed (or
    1 tsp garlic purée)
4–6 thin red chillies, finely
    chopped
1 tsp crushed dried chillies
1 tsp ground turmeric
1 tsp freshly ground black
    pepper
4 cardamom pods, split, seeds
    extracted
½ tsp ground cloves
½ tsp grated nutmeg
2 tsp grated fresh root ginger
    (or ginger purée)
3 tbsp sunflower oil
400ml water
700g pork leg, diced
150ml malt vinegar
1 tbsp soft light brown sugar
1 tsp salt
2 bay leaves

To serve
Plain Basmati Rice (page 128)
Carrot and Beetroot Salad
    with Mustard Yoghurt
    Dressing (page 146)

Preparation time:
10 minutes
Cooking time:
30 minutes
Freezable for:
3 months, without the pak choi

Serves 4 • Asian • 🌶🌶

Thai Pork Curry with Pak Choi

Ingredients:
400ml can of coconut milk
4 tbsp Thai green curry paste
2 tbsp Thai fish sauce
2 tsp soft light brown sugar
2 kaffir lime leaves
500g pork fillet, cubed
1 bunch of spring onions,
    cut into short lengths
4 baby pak choi
150ml boiling chicken stock
4 tomatoes, quartered
1 lime, quartered
1 fat red chilli, deseeded, if
    liked, and cut in thin
    strips

To serve
Perfect Thai Jasmine Rice
    (see page 129)

I have made slow cooker pork and spinach curry before, but this is an unusual variation in which braised baby pak choi are laid on top before serving. You can use quartered larger heads if you can't find the baby ones.

• Blend the coconut milk with the curry paste in a large saucepan. Add everything except the pak choi, stock, tomatoes, lime and chilli. Bring to the boil, reduce the heat, cover and simmer very gently for 30 minutes until the pork is really tender. Discard the lime leaves.

• Meanwhile, lay the pak choi in a frying pan. Pour over the boiling chicken stock, bring back to the boil, reduce the heat, cover and simmer gently for about 3 minutes or until just wilted but still with some bite. Drain the stock into the curry. Stir the tomatoes into the curry, too, and heat for a few minutes.

• Spoon the curry over jasmine rice in large bowls and top each with a baby pak choi and a few strips of red chilli. Finally garnish each with a lime wedge and serve.

Serves 4 • British • 🎵

Curried Slow-roast Pork Belly

Preparation time:
10 minutes plus marinating
Cooking time:
3½ hours
Not suitable for freezing

A curried rub spread all over the meat adds wonderful depth of flavour. Don't rub it on the crackling though or it won't crisp up! The slow cooking in stock and beer makes the meat meltingly tender too. The asafoetida gives added flavour, similar to leeks or onions.

- Mix the garlic with the spices, salt and 1 tbsp of the oil.

- Wipe the meat dry with kitchen paper then deeply score the skin in a criss-cross pattern.

- Rub the spice paste all over the flesh (but not the rind) and leave to marinate for at least 2 hours.

- Preheat the oven to 230°C/Gas 8.

- Put the pork in a roasting tin and rub the rind with the remaining oil and a little salt. Roast for about 20 minutes or until the crackling bubbles up.

- Reduce the heat to 150°C/Gas 2. Mix together the stock and lager with the honey and pour around the meat. Cook for a further 3 hours until meltingly tender.

- Remove the pork from the tin and leave to rest in a warm place for 10 minutes.

- Spoon off any excess fat from the tin, if necessary, then boil the juices rapidly until reduced and slightly thickened, stirring all the time. Taste and re-season, if necessary.

- Cut the meat into 4 thick slices, then each slice in 2 chunks. Arrange on plain rice or crushed new potatoes, spoon the juices over and serve with a crisp green salad.

Ingredients:
1 large garlic clove, crushed
1 tsp ground cumin
1 tsp ground coriander
2 tsp asafoetida (optional)
½ tsp chilli powder
¼ tsp ground cloves
1 tsp salt plus extra for the crackling
2 tbsp sunflower oil
900g pork belly in 1 piece
250ml beef stock
250ml bitter beer or lager
1 tbsp clear honey

To serve
Plain Basmati Rice (page 128) or crushed new potatoes
Crisp green salad

Preparation time:
10 minutes
Cooking time:
30 minutes
Freezable for:
1 month, without the spinach

Serves 4 • British • 🌶

Curried Pork Sausages with Potatoes on Wilted Spinach

Ingredients:
1 tbsp sunflower oil
1 onion, chopped (or 1 large handful of frozen chopped onion)
8 thick pork sausages, cut into chunks
2 tbsp Madras curry powder or paste
1 tsp ground turmeric
1 large garlic clove, crushed (or 1 tsp garlic purée)
12 waxy small salad potatoes (like Charlotte), halved
1 large bay leaf
450ml passata
1 tbsp tomato purée
4 tbsp boiling water
1 tsp caster sugar
½ tsp salt
400g spinach

To garnish
2 tbsp chopped fresh coriander

To serve
Chapattis (page 133) or use bought

Curried sausages may sound unusual, but this Anglo-Indian recipe makes a great supper dish and, surprisingly, is very tasty served cold too, if you have any left over! Use good-quality meaty, low-fat, coarse-textured sausages.

- Heat the oil in a large non-stick pan, add the onion and fry quickly for 3 minutes, stirring until golden. Remove from the pan. Add the sausage chunks and fry quickly on all sides to brown. Pour off any excess fat. Add the curry powder or paste and turmeric and fry for 30 seconds.

- Stir the remaining ingredients except the spinach into the pan and bring to the boil. Cover and simmer gently for 10 minutes.

- Remove the lid and simmer for a further 10 minutes until the potatoes are cooked through and everything is bathed in a rich sauce.

- Meanwhile, wash the spinach, shake off the excess water and cook in a pan without extra water, stirring, for 2–3 minutes until wilted. Drain thoroughly.

- Spoon the spinach into warm bowls, top with the sausage mixture, garnish with the chopped coriander and serve with chapattis.

Serves 4 • Asian • ♩♩

Thai Red Pork and Prawn Curry

Preparation time:
10 minutes
Cooking time:
10 minutes
Not suitable for freezing

This curry is simplicity itself to prepare and doesn't take long to cook either. The combination of pork and prawns has always been a favourite in Asian cooking as both are sweet-tasting and rich and complement one another perfectly.

- Heat the oil in a saucepan and fry the spring onions and pork for 2 minutes, stirring until the pork is no longer pink.

- Add the remaining ingredients except the mangetout and prawns. Bring to the boil, then reduce the heat and simmer gently for 5 minutes.

- Meanwhile, steam or boil the mangetout in water for 3 minutes until just tender. Drain, if necessary.

- Add the mangetout and prawns to the pork, stir and simmer for 3 minutes until the prawns are pink.

- Spoon over rice noodles in bowls, garnish with the coriander and serve.

Ingredients:
1 tbsp sunflower oil
1 bunch of spring onions, cut
   in short diagonal lengths
400g pork fillet, trimmed and
   diced
400ml can of coconut milk
4 tbsp Thai red curry paste
2 fat red chillies, deseeded
   and shredded
1 tsp soft light brown sugar
1 tbsp Thai fish sauce
100g mangetout, trimmed
200g raw peeled king prawns,
   tails left on

To garnish
2 tbsp chopped fresh
   coriander

To serve
Rice noodles

Preparation time:
25 minutes plus marinating
Cooking time:
35 minutes
Freezable for:
3 months

Serves 4 • Asian • ♪♪♪

Hot and Sour Prawn Curry

Ingredients:
2 tsp cumin seeds
1 tsp black mustard seeds
1 onion, roughly chopped
4 thin red chillies, deseeded,
   if liked, and chopped
4 cardamom pods, split,
   seeds extracted
2 tsp grated fresh root
   ginger (or ginger purée)
2 garlic cloves, chopped (or
   1 tsp garlic purée)
90ml red wine vinegar
1 tsp chilli powder
1 tsp ground cinnamon
1 tsp ground turmeric
600g pork fillet, diced
2 tbsp sunflower oil
400g can of chopped
   tomatoes
200ml water
Salt

To garnish
Chopped fresh coriander

To serve
Plain Basmati Rice (page
   128)
Large mixed salad

This is definitely a three-chilli curry for those who like it hot! Although you can always reduce the number of chillis or leave out the chilli powder if you want to let yourself in gently. Never be afraid to experiment to make the recipes exactly how you like them.

- In a dry frying pan, toast the cumin and mustard seeds for 30 seconds until fragrant. Tip into a mortar or a small food processor. Add the onion, chillies, cardamom seeds, ginger and garlic. Pound or blend to a paste, adding 1–2 tbsp of the vinegar. Add the chilli powder, cinnamon and turmeric.

- Spoon into a plastic container with a lid. Add the pork and toss well with your hands so it is all well coated in the paste. Ideally, cover and leave to marinate for several hours (or overnight if that suits you better).

- Heat the oil in a large heavy-based pan. Add the chicken and marinade and fry, stirring, for 2–3 minutes.

- Add the tomatoes, the remaining vinegar, the water and a little salt. Bring to the boil, reduce the heat and simmer gently for about 30 minutes, stirring occasionally, until rich, thick and the chicken is tender. Taste and re-season, if necessary.

- Garnish with fresh coriander and serve with plain basmati rice and a large mixed salad.

• Pork Curries

Serves 4–6 • Fusion • ♪♪

Preparation time:
20 minutes plus marinating
Cooking time:
1½ hours
Not suitable for freezing

East Meets West Spiced Pork Loin

The Cajun spices of Deep South cooking are blended with a touch of the East, with soy and sweet chilli sauces which combine to make a fabulous marinade for this tender pork loin, served with fragrant sweet potatoes and baby corn.

- Mix together the marinade ingredients, add the pork and turn to coat completely. Place in a sealable container and chill for at least 2 hours or preferably overnight.

- Preheat the oven to 180°C/Gas 4.

- Place the pork in an oiled roasting tin. Spoon the remaining marinade over each steak. Put the oil and rosemary in a separate tin. Add the sweet potatoes and baby corn and toss in the fragrant oil. Sprinkle with the salt. Pour the stock around the pork. Cover the tin with foil and place in the centre of the oven. Put the sweet potatoes and corn on the top shelf. Roast for 1½ hours until everything is really tender.

- Lift the pork out of the tin, wrap in foil on a plate and keep warm. Spoon off any fat from the pork cooking juices, then bring to the boil, and boil rapidly for 2–3 minutes, stirring, until slightly thickened and reduced.

- Serve the pork with the sweet potatoes and corn and spoon the reduced cooking juices over. Serve with roti breads or rolled flour tortillas and a beansprout salad.

To slow cook: Prepare the meat as above but put in the crock pot. Surround with the sweet potatoes tossed in the oil and the corn and cook on Low for 8 hours. Reduce the cooking juices as in the recipe.

To pressure cook: Not really suitable for pressure cooking.

Ingredients:
For the marinade
2 tbsp Cajun spice blend
Freshly ground black pepper
2 tbsp soy sauce
1 tbsp lime juice
4 tbsp sweet chilli sauce

For the pork
4 pork loin steaks
2 tbsp sunflower oil, plus extra for greasing
1 tbsp chopped fresh rosemary
2 large sweet potatoes, peeled and cut into bite-sized chunks
1 tsp coarse sea salt
100g baby sweetcorn
150ml pork or beef stock

To serve
Chinese egg noodles tossed in a splash of sesame oil
Beansprout and Black Mustard Seed Salad (page 143)

Vegetable and Pulse Curries

You don't have to be a vegetarian to enjoy these wonderful, colourful curries, packed with flavour and nutrients. Pulses (dried peas, beans and lentils) are great vehicles for all those intense spice flavours and provide protein and complex carbohydrates. Fresh vegetables, whether they be the starchy ones like potatoes and sweet potatoes; the robust roots like carrots and turnips; the sweet vegetable fruits like tomatoes and peppers; the legumes like peas and beans; or the wonderful, fresh, leafy greens, all have a valuable and delectable place in this whole array of dishes from around the world. Sometimes I've teamed them with other proteins, such as cheeses, eggs, or tofu so they all become complete, balanced meals. Some are more suitable for side dishes to accompany one of the meat or fish curries.

Serves 4 • Indian • ♪

Spinach and Potato Curry with Paneer and Eggs

Preparation time:
15 minutes
Cooking time:
20 minutes
Not suitable for freezing

Ingredients:
400g well-washed fresh or
  thawed frozen spinach
2 tbsp sunflower oil
1 large onion, halved and
  thinly sliced (or 2 large
  handfuls of frozen
  chopped onion)
1 large garlic clove, crushed
  (or 1 tsp garlic purée)
1 tsp ground cumin
½ tsp ground turmeric
2 large potatoes, peeled and
  cut into bite-sized chunks
1 red pepper, deseeded and
  cut in chunks
1 fat red chilli, deseeded and
  chopped
200ml water
Salt
2 tomatoes, quartered
200g paneer or Edam
  cheese, cubed
4 eggs

To garnish
1 tbsp lemon juice
2 tbsp torn coriander leaves

To serve
Naan breads (page 132) or
  use bought

This is *sag aloo* with additions! Obviously, for an accompaniment, simply omit the paneer and eggs but with them included, this curry makes a light and delicious simple lunch or supper dish.

• Squeeze the spinach, if using frozen, to remove excess moisture. Set aside.

• Heat the oil in a large saucepan. Add the onion and garlic and fry, stirring, for 2 minutes.

• Add the remaining ingredients except the spinach, tomatoes, paneer and eggs. Bring to the boil, reduce the heat, part-cover and simmer for 10 minutes.

• Add the spinach and tomatoes, stir gently, cover and cook for a further 5 minutes until the vegetables are tender but the tomatoes still have some shape.

• Stir in the paneer and cook a further 3 minutes.

• Taste and re-season if necessary. Spoon into bowls.

• Meanwhile, poach the eggs in gently simmering water with the lemon juice added until cooked to your liking. Carefully lift out with a draining spoon and place on top of the curry. Sprinkle with torn coriander leaves and serve with naan breads.

Serves 4 • Indian • 🌶

Mixed Vegetable Curry

Preparation time:
20 minutes
Cooking time:
25 minutes
Freezeable for:
6 months, although if you use a
lot of potato, the pieces may
be a little watery when thawed

The great thing about a vegetable curry is you can add any veggies you have to hand, from roots like turnips and swede to cauliflower, green beans or anything that takes your fancy. Experiment and enjoy on its own or as an accompaniment (in which case omit the chickpeas).

- Heat the oil in a large saucepan. Add the onion and garlic and fry, stirring, for 2 minutes.

- Add the spices and bay leaf or curry leaves and fry for 30 seconds. Stir in the coconut, water and tomato purée. Bring to the boil, stirring until the coconut has melted.

- Stir in the lemon juice and salt. Add all the vegetables and the raisins, if using. Stir gently. Bring back to the boil, reduce the heat, cover and simmer very gently for about 20 minutes, stirring occasionally, or until all the vegetables are tender and bathed in a rich sauce.

- Taste and re-season if necessary. Discard the bay leaf or curry leaves before serving, if liked.

Ingredients:
2 tbsp sunflower oil
1 large garlic clove, crushed
  (or ½ tsp garlic purée)
1 large onion, chopped (or a
  large handful of frozen
  chopped onion)
2 tsp Madras curry powder or
  paste
1 tbsp garam masala
¼ tsp chilli powder (optional)
1 bay leaf (or 2 curry leaves)
120g creamed coconut, cut in
  small pieces
450ml water
2 tbsp tomato purée (paste)
1 tbsp lemon juice
1 tsp salt
1 large carrot, sliced
¼ cabbage, shredded
1 small green pepper, cut in
  chunks
1 large potato, peeled and cut
  in chunks
400g can of chickpeas,
  drained
75g frozen peas
Handful of raisins (optional)

Preparation time:
15 minutes
Cooking time:
25 minutes
Freezable for:
3 months

Serves 4 • British • 🌶🌶

Pumpkin and White Bean Curry

Ingredients:
2 tbsp sunflower oil
1 large onion, halved and
    thinly sliced
2 tbsp black mustard seeds
1 tsp cumin seeds
2 curry leaves
4 cardamom pods, split,
    seeds extracted
1 tsp ground turmeric
½ tsp chilli powder
1 tsp garam masala
1 tsp soft light brown sugar
400g can of haricot beans,
    drained
250ml vegetable stock
1 small pumpkin or a large
    wedge, about 700g,
    peeled, deseeded and cut
    into bite-sized chunks
400g can of chopped
    tomatoes
Salt

To serve
Carrot Raita (page 136)
Chapattis (page 133) or use
    bought
Green salad

When pumpkin isn't available, you can use any other orange-fleshed winter squash instead. The recipe also works well with sweet potatoes. You can add chickpeas or lentils instead of white beans to ring the changes.

- Heat the oil in a frying pan, add the onion and fry, stirring, for 4 minutes until lightly golden. Stir in the mustard and cumin seeds and cook until they start to pop.

- Add the curry leaves and remaining spices and stir for 30 seconds. Add remaining ingredients, seasoning with a little salt. Bring to the boil, reduce the heat, part-cover and simmer gently for 20 minutes until the pumpkin is tender.

- Discard the curry leaves, if liked, stir gently and serve in bowls, topped with carrot raita, with chapattis and a green salad.

• Vegetable and Pulse Curries

Preparation time:
10 minutes plus soaking
Cooking time:
35 minutes
Freezeable for:
3 months

Mushroom and Soya Bean Curry with Almonds

Soya (edamame) beans are also sold in their pods, which are cooked and then the beans popped out of the pods straight into the mouth as a snack. Here I've used readily available frozen soya beans as a source of protein, colour and texture in this Chinese-style curry.

- Soak the shiitake mushrooms in the warm water for 30 minutes.

- Heat the oil in a large pan. Add the seeds and fry until they start to pop.

- Add the onion and fry, stirring, for 2 minutes. Stir in the garlic, ginger and curry powder and fry for 30 seconds.

- Add the chestnut mushrooms, the soaked mushrooms and their water, the tomatoes and the soya beans. Season with the soy sauce and stir well. Bring to the boil, reduce the heat and simmer gently for 30 minutes.

- Blend the cornflour with the water and stir in. Bring to the boil, stirring until thickened and clear. Cook for 1 minute more, stirring. Taste and re-season, if necessary with a little more soy sauce.

- Serve spooned over plain boiled rice, with the coriander or mint and almonds scattered over, with a crisp green salad.

Ingredients:
2 tbsp dried sliced shiitake
   mushrooms
150ml warm water
2 tbsp sunflower oil
1 tbsp black mustard seeds
1 large onion, chopped (or
   2 large handfuls of frozen
   chopped onion)
2 garlic cloves, crushed (or
   1 tsp garlic purée)
1 tsp grated fresh root ginger
   (or ginger purée)
2 tbsp Madras curry powder
   or paste
400g chestnut mushrooms,
   quartered
400g can of chopped
   tomatoes
200g frozen shelled soya
   beans
1 tbsp soy sauce
2 tbsp chopped fresh
   coriander or mint
25g toasted flaked almonds
3 tbsp cornflour
4 tbsp water

To serve
Plain Basmati Rice (page 128)
Green salad

Preparation time:
15 minutes
Cooking time:
20 minutes
Not suitable for freezing

Serves 4 • Indian • ♪♪

Bombay Potatoes

Ingredients:
700g potatoes, peeled and
   cut in walnut-sized pieces
Salt
2 tbsp sunflower oil
2 thin green chillies,
   deseeded, if liked, and
   finely chopped
1 tsp ground cumin
1 tsp ground coriander
¼ tsp ground turmeric
400g can of chopped
   tomatoes
Good pinch of caster sugar
2 tbsp chopped fresh or
   frozen coriander

Bombay aloo is a particular favourite as a snack or starter (try the pieces speared on cocktail sticks with a carrot or cucumber raita (pages 136–7) or some mango chutney to dip into) or as an accompaniment to any curry for a change from rice. Alternatively, top it with some fried eggs.

- Boil the potatoes in lightly salted water for about 10 minutes until just tender but still holding their shape. Drain.

- Meanwhile, heat the oil in a large non-stick pan and fry the spices, over a moderate heat, stirring for 30 seconds. Add the tomatoes and sugar, stir, then fry for 2–3 minutes.

- Add the potatoes and stir and turn gently until the potatoes are coated in the spicy tomatoes. Sprinkle with just a little salt. Cover with a lid, reduce the heat and cook for about 10 minutes, stirring occasionally so the potatoes don't stick to the pan. Add the coriander and stir and turn one more time. Serve hot.

Serves 4 • Indian • 🍌

Preparation time:
15 minutes
Cooking time:
25–35 minutes
Not suitable for freezing

Cauliflower, Potato and Paneer Curry

Gobi aloo is a popular dish in Northern India where it is usually served as an accompaniment to a main course. I've added the paneer to make it a more substantial main course dish but you can omit if serving as an accompaniment.

- Heat the oil in a large saucepan, add the cumin seeds and fry for 30 seconds. Add the onion and fry, stirring, for 3 minutes. Add the remaining spices, the garlic, tomatoes and sugar and stir for 1 minute.

- Add the potatoes and cauliflower and stir until coated in the mixture. Stir in stock and seasoning to taste. Bring to the boil, reduce the heat and simmer gently for 20–30 minutes until really tender and everything is bathed in a rich sauce.

- Gently stir in the paneer and heat for 1 minute. Taste and re-season, if necessary. Garnish with the chives or spring onion and serve hot with chapattis and a mixed salad.

Ingredients:
2 tbsp sunflower oil
1 tsp cumin seeds
1 large onion, halved and thinly sliced
2 cardamom pods, split, seeds extracted
1 tbsp sweet paprika
½ tsp ground turmeric
1 tsp grated fresh root ginger (or ginger purée)
1 thin green chilli, deseeded, and finely chopped
1 large garlic clove, crushed (or 1 tsp garlic purée)
3 tomatoes, skinned, deseeded and chopped
1 tsp soft light brown sugar
2 large potatoes, peeled and cut into bite-sized chunks
1 small cauliflower, cut into small florets
200ml vegetable stock
200g paneer, diced
Salt and freshly ground black pepper

To garnish
A few snipped chives or chopped spring onion

To serve
Chapattis (page 133) or use bought
Mixed Salad with Cumin and Onion Seed Dressing (page 141)

Serves 4 • Fusion • ♪

Roasted Sweetcorn in Curried Butter

Ingredients:
4 corn cobs in their husks
50 g softened butter, cut
   into small pieces
2 tbsp Madras curry powder
   or paste
1 tbsp tomato purée
1 tbsp mango chutney

When fresh cobs in their husks aren't available, simply use thawed frozen ones and wrap them in foil with the buttery mixture smeared over them. This is a delicious dish that does not pretend to be authentic but really works.

- Preheat the oven to 180°C/Gas 4.

- Pull back the husks gently and remove the silks from the corn cobs but leave the husks intact. Rinse to remove any loose silks and pat dry.

- Mash the butter with the curry powder or paste, tomato purée and mango chutney. Gently smear the butter mixture around the corn between the kernels and the husks. Fold the husks back over the butter.

- Lay the corn in a shallow baking dish. Bake in the oven for 30 minutes until tender.

- Carefully lift the corn out of the dish onto plates. Remove the husks and serve with the residual melted butter mixture from the tin spooned over.

Serves 4 • Fusion • 🌙

Curried Green Beans with Tomatoes

Preparation time:
10 minutes
Cooking time:
8 minutes
Freezeable for:
3 months

These are a delicious accompaniment to any Indian or Caribbean-style curry. Like most of the vegetable curries, they can be turned into a light meal with the addition of a little protein in the form of diced tofu or hard-boiled egg. They are also good spooned into plain omelettes.

Ingredients:
200g green beans, topped and tailed
Salt and freshly ground black pepper
Large knob of butter
2 spring onions, chopped
1 fat red chilli, deseeded, if liked, and finely chopped
1 tsp ground cumin
1 tsp garam masala
4 tbsp water
100g cherry tomatoes, halved
A good pinch of caster sugar
Salt and freshly ground black pepper

- Cook the beans in lightly salted water for 3 minutes only until almost tender but still a little crunchy. Drain and rinse with cold water.

- Melt the butter in the saucepan. Add the spring onions and spices and fry for 1 minute, stirring.

- Add the water, tomatoes and sugar and simmer for 3 minutes until the tomatoes are hot through but still hold their shape. Return the beans to the pan and toss well to heat through. Season to taste. Serve hot.

Preparation time:
10 minutes
Cooking time:
10 minutes
Freezable for:
3 months

Serves 4 • Caribbean • 𝄞

Curried Kale with Sweetcorn and Peanuts

Ingredients:
400ml vegetable stock
400g kale, shredded,
    discarding thick stumps
200g fresh or frozen
    sweetcorn kernels
2 tbsp Madras curry powder
    or paste
1 tbsp lemon juice
Handful of sultanas
Salt and freshly ground black
    pepper
Large knob of butter
5 tbsp desiccated coconut
50g roasted unsalted
    peanuts
½ tsp garam masala

To serve
Plain Basmati Rice (page
    128)

This makes a delicious light lunch or supper dish. The peanuts and sweetcorn add texture, flavour and a little protein for a simple meal. If you have fresh corn cobs, simply hold them upright firmly on a board then cut downwards all round to cut off the kernels.

● Bring the stock to the boil in a large pan. Stir in the kale, bring back to the boil, cover and cook for 4 minutes until just tender. Do not overcook. Drain, reserving the stock. Set the vegetables aside.

● Pour the stock back into the pan and stir in the curry paste, lemon juice, sultanas, a little salt and plenty of black pepper. Bring to the boil, whisk in the butter and boil rapidly until well reduced and slightly thickened, about 5 minutes.

● Meanwhile, toast the coconut in a non-stick frying pan, stirring all the time until lightly browned, about 2 minutes. Tip onto a plate.

● Stir the kale and sweetcorn, peanuts and garam masala into the reduced curry sauce. Toss over a fairly high heat until piping hot.

● Spoon onto plates, dust with the coconut. Spoon onto plain basmati rice and serve.

● Vegetable and Pulse Curries

Serves 4 • Indian • 𝄞𝄞

Baby Aubergine, Tomato and Celeriac Curry

Preparation time:
20 minutes
Cooking time:
34 minutes
Freezeable for:
3 months, without the chickpeas

Baby aubergines are perfect for the curry treatment and they are available in larger supermarkets, but if you can't find any, simply use a large aubergine and cut it into thick finger-length pieces.

- Heat the oil in a large saucepan, add the onion and fry quickly, stirring, for 3 minutes until softened and lightly golden.

- Add half the garlic and the spices and fry for 30 seconds. Stir in the tomatoes, stock, sugar and some salt and pepper and bring to the boil, stirring.

- Add the aubergines and celeriac, season, bring back to the boil, reduce the heat to moderate, cover and simmer for 15 minutes.

- Remove the lid and simmer for a further 15 minutes or until the vegetables are tender and the sauce is reduced.

- Meanwhile, melt the butter in a non-stick pan. Add the remaining garlic and the drained peas. Crush gently with a potato masher or the back of a wooden spoon – they should be broken up but not pulpy. Season to taste and add half the coriander. Heat through, stirring.

- Discard the cinnamon stick, star anise and bay leaf from the curry. Stir the remaining coriander into the yoghurt.

- Spoon the crushed peas onto plates and spoon the curry over. Top with a good dollop of the coriander yoghurt and serve.

Ingredients:
2 tbsp sunflower oil
1 large onion, chopped (or 2 large handfuls of frozen chopped onion)
2 large garlic cloves, crushed (or 1½ tsp garlic purée)
2 fat red chillies, deseeded, if liked, and chopped
1 tsp crushed dried chillies (optional)
1 tsp ground cumin
1 piece of cinnamon stick
1 bay leaf
1 star anise
400g can of chopped tomatoes
300ml vegetable stock
½ tsp soft light brown sugar
Salt and freshly ground black pepper
8 baby aubergines, trimmed and halved lengthways
1 small celeriac, cut in 1cm thick slices, then fingers
25g butter
2 x 400g cans of chickpeas or black eyed peas, drained
3 tbsp chopped fresh or frozen coriander
120ml thick plain yoghurt

Preparation time:
15 minutes
Cooking time:
40 minutes
Freezable for:
3 months, without the garam masala or cheese

Serves 4 • fusion • ♩

Courgette Curry with Feta and Baked Rice

Ingredients:
4 tbsp olive oil, plus extra for drizzling
2 large courgettes, thickly sliced
1 onion, finely chopped (or a large handful of frozen chopped onion)
1 tsp ground cumin
1 tsp ground cinnamon
1 tsp crushed dried chillies
400g can of chopped tomatoes
4 tbsp kalamata olives, halved and stoned
1 tsp dried oregano
½ tsp caster sugar
Salt and freshly ground black pepper
225g basmati rice
1 bay leaf
500ml boiling vegetable stock or water
2 tsp garam masala
150g Feta cheese, cubed

To serve
Warm pitta breads (or naans)
Mixed Salad with Cumin and Onion Seed Dressing (page 141)

This is Greece meets India! It's a delicious blend of the two and I really like it served with warm pitta breads but you could go the other way and serve it with naans. The Indian salad is a great accompaniment for this curry.

- Preheat the oven to 180°C/Gas 4.

- Heat the oil in a flameproof casserole. Add the courgettes and fry until golden on both sides. Remove with a draining spoon and set aside.

- Add the onion to the casserole and fry for 2 minutes.

- Stir in the spices and fry for 30 seconds. Add the tomatoes, olives, oregano, sugar, and season lightly (you are going to be adding salty Feta later). Add the courgettes. Stir gently, bring to the boil, drizzle with a little extra olive oil, cover and cook in the oven for 30 minutes.

- Meanwhile, wash the rice, drain well and put in a separate casserole dish. Add the bay leaf and a good pinch of salt. Pour the boiling stock or water over, and stir in half the garam masala. Cover with foil then the lid and put in the oven. Bake for 30 minutes. Remove from the oven, take off the lid and leave undisturbed for a few minutes, then fluff up with a fork.

- Stir the garam masala and Feta into the curry and return to the oven for 5 minutes.

- Remove the lid and foil from the rice, fluff up and spoon into bowls. Top with the curry and serve with pitta breads (or naans) and a mixed salad.

Serves 4 • Indian • 🌙

Spiced Red Lentils with Fried Onions

Preparation time:
10 minutes
Cooking time:
25–30 minutes
Freezeable for:
6 months

Masoor dal is made with red lentils, which need no pre-soaking, so is quick to prepare. It's perfect to serve as an accompaniment but is also good with cubes of paneer or tofu folded through just before serving with naan bread and a green salad for a delicious lunch or supper.

- Put the lentils in a large saucepan with the garlic, turmeric, asafoetida and ginger. Add the stock or water. Stir well, bring to the boil, reduce the heat, cover and simmer for 25–30 minutes until pulpy and the water has been absorbed, stirring occasionally.

- After 15 minutes, heat the butter or ghee in a small pan. Add the onion and fry for about 5 minutes, stirring until golden and cooked through.

- Stir in the remaining ingredients except the salt and onion seeds and fry for 30 seconds. Remove from the heat.

- When the lentils are cooked, stir in the onion mixture, season to taste with salt, sprinkle with the black onions seeds and serve hot.

Ingredients:
175g red lentils
1 garlic clove, crushed (or ½ tsp garlic purée)
1 tsp ground turmeric
1 tsp asafoetida (optional)
1 tsp grated fresh root ginger (or ginger purée)
500ml chicken or vegetable stock, or water
30g butter or ghee
1 onion, sliced (or a large handful of frozen chopped onion)
1 tsp ground cumin
1 tsp ground coriander
2 tsp sweet paprika
1 tsp crushed dried chillies
1 tsp garam masala
1 tsp black onion seeds
Salt

Preparation time:
10 minutes plus soaking
Cooking time:
35–45 minutes
Freezable for:
3 months

Serves 4 • Indian • ♪

Yellow Split Peas with Onions and Red Chilli

Ingredients:
175g yellow split peas, soaked in cold water for several hours or overnight
600ml boiling water
2 tbsp sunflower oil
Large knob of butter
1 tsp ground cumin
1 tsp ground coriander
1 tsp grated fresh root ginger (or ginger purée)
¼ tsp ground turmeric
¼ tsp asafoetida (optional)
2 tomatoes, skinned and chopped
2 large onions, halved and thinly sliced
2 fat red chillies, deseeded, and cut in thin strips
Salt and freshly ground black pepper

My version of *tarka dal* is particularly tasty with the addition of the tomatoes. Serve it to accompany curries, of course, but it's also lovely just with flavoured naan breads or chapattis for a light lunch, with a crisp salad.

- Drain the soaked split peas and place in a saucepan. Cover with the boiling water, bring to the boil, reduce the heat, cover and simmer gently for 35–45 minutes until tender and the water is absorbed, stirring occasionally.

- Meanwhile, heat the oil and butter in a frying pan, add the onions and fry, stirring, for 5 minutes until soft and golden.

- Add the remaining ingredients and cook, stirring, for a further 5 minutes.

- Gently stir the onion spice mixture into the dal and season to taste. Serve hot.

Serves 4 • Indian • ♪

Dal in a Rush

Preparation time:
5 minutes
Cooking time:
5 minutes
Not suitable for freezing

This almost instant dal can accompany any Indian-style curry but is also delicious spread on naan breads with some shredded lettuce and a sprinkling of lemon juice, for a quick snack. You can also thin it with stock and serve as a soup.

Ingredients:
410g can of pease pudding
6 tbsp water
1 tbsp smooth mango chutney
3 tbsp sunflower oil
1 onion, chopped (or a large handful of frozen chopped onion)
1 tsp garam masala
¼ tsp chilli powder
Salt

- Empty the contents of the can of pease pudding into a non-stick pan. Add the water. Break up the peas pudding and heat, stirring, until piping hot.

- Stir in the mango chutney.

- Meanwhile, heat the oil in a frying pan and fry the onion, stirring, for 3–4 minutes until golden and soft. Stir in the garam masala and chilli powder and fry for 30 seconds, stirring.

- Add to the pease pudding and stir well. Season to taste with salt. Serve hot.

Preparation time:
10 minutes
Cooking time:
22 minutes
Not suitable for freezing

Serves 4 • Asian • ♪

Tofu, Sugarsnap Pea and Sweet Potato Green Curry

Ingredients:
1 tbsp sunflower oil
4 spring onions, cut in short
   lengths
1 sweet potato, peeled and
   cut in walnut-sized pieces
3 tbsp Thai green curry paste
400ml can of coconut milk
1 tbsp Thai fish sauce
350g block firm tofu, dried
   on kitchen paper and
   cubed
225g sugarsnap peas
2 tomatoes, quartered
5cm piece of cucumber,
   peeled, deseeded and cut
   in matchsticks
A few torn parsley or mint
   leaves

To serve
Perfect Thai Jasmine Rice
   (page 129)

The addition of some tomatoes and cucumber at the end add delicious extra textures and flavours. You can use ordinary potato if you don't like sweet potato but you'll need to simmer it for at least 10 minutes to cook it before adding the remaining ingredients.

• Heat the oil in a large saucepan or wok. Add the spring onions and fry, stirring, for 2 minutes until lightly coloured.

• Add the sweet potatoes and cook, stirring for 1 minute.

• Stir in the curry paste, coconut milk and Thai fish sauce. Bring to the boil, reduce the heat, cover and simmer, stirring occasionally, for 6–7 minutes or until the sweet potatoes are nearly tender.

• Add the tofu, cover and simmer very gently for a further 10 minutes.

• Meanwhile steam the sugarsnap peas over a pan of simmering water for about 3 minutes until just tender.

• Stir them into the curry and add the quartered tomatoes and cucumber strips. Simmer for 2 minutes until the tomatoes are softened slightly but still hold their shape.

• Spoon the curry over jasmine rice in bowls and garnish with a few torn parsley or mint leaves.

• Vegetable and Pulse Curries

Serves 4 • Indian • 🌙

Curried Vegetable Naan Pizza

Preparation time:
10 minutes
Cooking time:
12–15 minutes
Not suitable for freezing

Naan breads make ideal spicy pizza bases. Here they are topped with a tomato and curry sauce and vegetables for a delicious snack meal. If you use my small home-made naans (page 132) you could probably want a couple per person!

- Preheat the oven to 200°C/Gas 6.

- Put the naans on 2 baking sheets.

- Mix the curry paste with the tomato purée, soft cheese and mango chutney. Spread over the naans. Scatter the peppers and mushrooms over, then drizzle with a little of the pepper oil and sprinkle with the Mozzarella cheese.

- Bake in the oven for 12–15 minutes until bubbling and the cheese is turning golden. Serve hot with a crisp green salad.

Ingredients:
4 large plain naan breads
4 tbsp Madras curry paste
2 tbsp tomato purée
4 tbsp soft white cheese
1 tbsp mango chutney
280g jar roasted peppers in oil antipasti, drained, reserving the oil
4 chestnut mushrooms, sliced
150g Mozzarella cheese, grated

To serve
Crisp green salad

Preparation time:
15 minutes
Cooking time:
30 minutes
Freezable for:
6 months

Serves 4 • Indian • ♪

Aubergine, Lentil and Pea Curry

Ingredients:
8 small waxy potatoes, quartered
1 large aubergine, diced
3 tbsp sunflower oil
1 large onion, chopped (or 2 large handfuls of frozen chopped onion)
1 garlic clove, crushed (or ½ tsp garlic purée)
2 tbsp Madras curry powder or paste
1 tbsp tomato purée
1 tbsp mango chutney
225g frozen peas
200ml vegetable stock
150ml plain yoghurt
2 x 400g cans of green lentils, drained
Salt
2 tbsp chopped coriander, to garnish

To serve
Chapattis (page 133) or use bought

A delicious, chunky curry suitable for any occasion, you can soak and boil 200g dried brown or green lentils instead of using the cans if you prefer. If you do that, cook twice as many (to save fuel) and freeze for up to 12 months.

- Heat the oil in a large saucepan. Add the onion and garlic and fry, stirring, for 4–5 minutes until golden.

- Stir in the aubergine and fry, stirring, for 2 minutes to soften slightly and absorb the excess oil.

- Add all the remaining ingredients. Season to taste, bring to the boil, reduce the heat and simmer gently for 30 minutes until the aubergine is tender and everything is bathed in a rich sauce.

- Taste and re-season if necessary. Spoon into bowls and sprinkle with the coriander.

- Serve with chapattis to scoop up the curry.

• Vegetable and Pulse Curries

Stir-fried Mangetout with Spring Onions

This is a really nice side dish for you to serve with any of the lighter, coconut-based curries. You can use the same recipe but substituting sugarsnap peas or sticks of courgette for the mangetout if you like and stir-fry for a minute or two longer.

- Heat the oil in a frying pan or wok. Add the spring onions and stir-fry for 2 minutes.

- Add the mangetout and stir-fry for 2 minutes.

- Add the remaining ingredients and toss and stir-fry for 1 minute more. Serve hot.

Ingredients:
2 tbsp sunflower oil
1 bunch of spring onions, cut in short lengths
150g mangetout, trimmed
1 tsp grated fresh root ginger (or ginger purée)
1 garlic clove, finely chopped (or ½ tsp garlic purée)
1 fat red chilli, deseeded and cut into thin rings
½ tsp soft light brown sugar
1 tbsp light soy sauce

Rice and Other Accompaniments

When you have a curry, you may think you always have to have rice. It is true that for many dishes, the rice acts as the perfect vehicle to hold the curry and to soak up the lovely sauce or juice. So here I've given you some of the best rice accompaniments whether for Thai food or Indian dishes. You may just want to cook plain basmati, in which case I've given you the most fail-safe method, or just follow the packet directions (or buy quick-cook or microwave rice, whatever you normally do). But, apart from rice, you might like to try some easy-to-make flat breads, whether from India or from the Caribbean. They're great for wiping up the sauce or for rolling up and using as a scoop.

As it's important to top up your five-a-day, I've also included some refreshing salads, with appropriate flavours designed to accompany dishes from different parts of the globe. In the pulse and vegetable curry chapter, you'll also find some great curries that can be served as side dishes or mains. Here you'll also find a few taste-tingling relishes and sauces to enhance the flavour of any of the curries or to act as dips for some of the starters. They're all the extra bits you need to enhance your meal.

Preparation time:
3 minutes
Cooking time:
15 minutes plus standing
Freezable for:
6 months

Serves 4 • Indian

Plain Basmati Rice

Ingredients:
300ml basmati rice
2 good pinches of salt
600ml boiling water or stock

Many people have a problem cooking rice. This is the simplest and most fool-proof method I know to ensure fluffy separate grains every time. Just use your measuring jug for the rice and the liquid, then it's easy to measure exactly the right amount you wish to cook.

- Measure the rice in a measuring jug and place it in a saucepan. Add the salt. Measure the boiling water or stock in the same jug and pour it into the pan. Stir just once to separate the grains.

- Bring back to the boil, then cover tightly with a lid. Turn down the heat as low as possible and leave untouched for 15 minutes. Do not be tempted to take off the lid or stir again during cooking.

- Remove from the heat, take off the lid, cover the pan with a double sheet of kitchen paper or a clean cloth and leave to stand undisturbed for 5 minutes.

- Fluff the rice up with a fork before serving.

Perfect Thai Jasmine Rice

Preparation time:
3 minutes
Cooking time:
20 minutes plus standing time
Not suitable for freezing

Thai rice should be slightly sticky but not soggy and wet. This is the best method to get excellent results to mop up all those lovely runny curries. For the record, Thai fragrant rice is just lower grade Jasmine rice and can be used instead.

Ingredients:
375ml water
Salt
225g jasmine rice

- Put the measured water in a large saucepan with a good pinch of salt and bring to the boil.
- Add the rice, stir, bring back to the boil, cover, reduce the heat, cover tightly and simmer gently for 20 minutes.
- Remove from the heat and leave to stand for 5 minutes.
- Remove the lid and stir gently with a fork before serving.

Preparation time:
5 minutes
Cooking time:
20 minutes plus standing time
Freezable for:
6 months

Serves 4 • **Indian**

Simple Yellow Pilau Rice

Ingredients:
225g basmati rice
550ml water
2 tbsp sunflower oil
4 cardamom pods, split
1 piece of cinnamon stick
4 cloves
1 tsp ground turmeric
1 chicken or vegetable stock
   cube or 1 tbsp stock
   concentrate
Freshly ground black pepper

For Brown Pilau rice, simply use brown basmati rice and cook for about 30 minutes instead of 20 and leave to stand, covered, as in the recipe. For non-coloured rice, omit the turmeric.

• Soak the rice in the water and set aside.

• Heat the oil in a heavy-based saucepan and fry the spices for 30 seconds, stirring.

• Add the rice and soaking water. Crumble in the stock cube, or add the concentrate, a pinch of salt and a good grinding of pepper. Bring to the boil, reduce the heat as low as possible, cover tightly with foil then the lid and cook for 20 minutes.

• Leave to stand for 5 minutes, then remove the lid and fluff up with a fork. If necessary, cover again and keep warm until ready to serve (the rice becomes fluffier and drier if it stands a little longer).

Preparat.
10 m,.
Cooking time.
20 or 30 minutes plus standing time
Freezeable for:
6 months

Baked Mushroom Pilau Rice

This dish can be baked at a higher temperature for a shorter time (for when cooking the Tandoori Chicken, for example) or at a lower temperature for longer (when cooking other curries or casseroles in the oven). It also makes a great dish on its own, served with some dal.

Ingredients:
2 tbsp sunflower oil
1 onion, finely chopped (or a large handful of frozen chopped onion)
2 garlic cloves, crushed (or 1 tsp garlic purée)
2 tsp grated fresh root ginger (or ginger purée)
¼ tsp chilli powder
1 tsp garam masala
250g basmati rice
175g chestnut mushrooms, thickly sliced
500ml hot chicken or vegetable stock
Pinch of salt

- Preheat the oven to 220°C/Gas 7 or 180°C/Gas 4, depending on which curry you are baking.

- Heat the oil in a flameproof casserole and gently fry the onion, stirring, for 2 minutes until softened but not browned.

- Stir in the garlic, ginger, chilli and garam masala and fry 30 seconds. Stir in the rice until all the grains are glistening.

- Add the mushrooms, stock and salt. Bring to the boil, stir, cover and cook in the oven for 20 minutes at the higher temperature or 30 minutes at the lower temperature until the rice is just tender and the liquid is almost absorbed.

- Remove from the oven but do not uncover. Leave to stand for 5 minutes.

- Remove the lid, let the steam escape for a minute or so, then fluff up with a fork. Remove the bay leaf and spices, if liked, before serving.

Makes about 8 breads • Indian

Quick Coriander and Garlic Naans

Ingredients:
250g self-raising flour
175ml plain yoghurt
1½ tbsp sunflower oil
½ tsp caster sugar
½ tsp salt
1 egg, beaten
60g butter, softened
2 tbsp chopped fresh or
  frozen coriander
2 garlic cloves, crushed (or
  1 tsp garlic purée)

If you prefer plain naan without the flavouring, simply don't add the butter mixture after cooking. You can use the same garlic and coriander butter to sandwich slices of baguette together, wrap in foil and bake in the oven for 15 minutes.

- Mix all the ingredients except the butter, coriander and garlic to form a soft dough. Knead gently on a lightly floured surface until smooth then divide the mixture into 8 balls.

- Preheat the oven to 220°C/Gas 7.

- Roll out the dough to rounds about the size of your hand and pull one edge to make them pear-shaped.

- Place on non-stick baking sheets and brush with a little water. Bake in the oven for about 8 minutes until puffy and browning slightly.

- Meanwhile, mash the butter with the coriander, garlic and a pinch of salt. Spread over the naans and return to the switched-off oven for a couple of minutes until the butter has soaked into the breads.

- Serve warm.

Makes 6 small or 4 large • Indian

Chapattis

Preparation time:
15 minutes plus resting
Cooking time:
12 minutes
Freezeable for:
6 months, interleaved with
greaseproof paper or baking
parchment

You can buy these in most supermarkets but they are very simple to make at home. If you don't have wholemeal flour, you could make them just as easily with plain flour (using a little less water) but the texture won't be as good.

Ingredients:
225g wholemeal flour
¾ tsp salt
250ml cold water
A little sunflower oil, melted butter or ghee for greasing

- Mix the flour and salt in a bowl. Stir in enough of the water to form a soft but not sticky dough. Knead gently on a lightly floured surface until smooth and elastic. Wrap in clingfilm and leave to rest for at least 15 minutes.

- Shape the dough into 4–6 balls. Keep them covered with a damp cloth.

- Heat a heavy non-stick frying pan and lightly grease with oil, butter or ghee. Roll out one ball on a lightly floured surface a round as thin as possible.

- Cook the chapatti quickly until the edges begin to curl and lightly browning in places. Flip over and cook the other side briefly. Remove and wrap in a napkin and keep warm.

- Repeat with all the remaining pieces of dough, adding each to the napkin as you go.

- Serve hot with any curry. Tear off pieces and use to scoop up the food.

Preparation time:
2 minutes
Cooking time:
8 minutes
Not suitable for freezing

Serves 4 • Indian

Popadoms

Ingredients:
4 plain dried popadoms
4 with chilli or cumin dried
popadoms

To serve
Fresh Mango Chutney (page
138) or use bought
Cucumber Raita (page 137)
Lime pickle

Ready-cooked popadoms have been fried and can be quite greasy. For healthier (and cheaper) ones, buy packs of dried popadoms (plain, with chilli or cumin). They keep for months in the cupboard even when opened. Serve with Indian dips to nibble before a meal or as an accompaniment to Indian-style curries.

• Separate the popadoms carefully (they are very fragile).

• Place one at a time on the microwave turntable and cook for about 30 seconds each side on full power until they puff up all over. You may need to rotate them on the turntable to ensure every bit puffs up.

• Place in a shallow basket and cook the remainder in the same way. (They can be made up to a couple of hours in advance.)

• Store any uneaten ones in an airtight container for up to a couple of weeks, then, if necessary, refresh in the microwave for 20 seconds before eating.

• **Rice and Other Accompaniments**

Caribbean Roti Breads

10 mi

Preparati
5 min
Not

6 montl...,
greaseproof paper or baking
parchment

These light, tasty breads are delicious with any curry. They make a perfect quick bread to go with African, Thai or, of course, Caribbean-style ones but are also a nice change from chapattis or naans with Indian dishes.

Ingredients:
- 100g gram (chickpea) flour
- 100g plain flour
- 2 tsp baking powder
- ½ tsp salt
- 30g unsalted butter, cut in small pieces
- 1 egg, beaten
- A little water

- Sift the flours, baking powder and salt together in a bowl. Add the butter and rub in with the fingertips. Mix with the egg and enough water to form a a soft but not sticky dough. Knead gently until smooth, then wrap in clingfilm and chill for at least 1 hour.

- Divide into 8 equal pieces then roll out to circles about 15cm diameter.

- Heat a non-stick heavy frying pan and fry each circle until it starts to puff up and brown slightly underneath. Flip over and cook the other side briefly. Wrap in a cloth and keep warm whilst cooking the remainder. Serve warm.

Serves 4 • Indian

Carrot Raita

Ingredients:

150ml thick plain yoghurt
1 carrot, coarsely grated
2 tbsp fresh chopped
  coriander
1 small green chilli,
  deseeded, if liked, and
  finely chopped
Salt and freshly ground black
  pepper

A refreshing accompaniment, especially to hot curries, you can reduce the heat by cutting back on the chilli, or omitting it altogether. The carrot gives this raita a lovely colour and texture – just slightly crunchy and very cooling.

- Put the yoghurt in a small bowl.

- Stir in the carrot, coriander and chilli and season with salt and pepper to taste.

- Chill until ready to serve.

Cucumber Raita

Preparation time:
5 minutes
Not suitable for freezing

Total refreshment, this is perfect to cool down any hot curries, or to serve with popadoms and pickles to whet the appetite for the meal to come. You can peel the cucumber if you wish but I leave the skin on for more colour and texture.

Ingredients:
150ml thick plain yoghurt
5cm piece cucumber, grated
  or finely chopped
2 tbsp fresh chopped mint
Salt and freshly ground black
  pepper

- Put the yoghurt in a small bowl.
- Stir in the cucumber and mint and season with salt and pepper to taste.
- Chill until ready to serve.

Serves 4–6 • Indian

Fresh Mango Chutney

Ingredients:
1 ripe mango
3 tbsp clear honey
2 tsp white wine vinegar
1 tsp grated fresh root
  ginger (or ginger purée)
½ garlic clove (or ¼ tsp
  garlic purée)
½ tsp tamarind paste

This is not a cooked, preserved chutney but makes a delicious accompaniment to any curry – particularly Indian-style ones – and will keep for several days in the fridge (or can be frozen). You can eat straight away but it is even better the next day!

- Peel the mango and cut all the fruit off the stone. Purée half in a blender or food processor with the honey and vinegar. Finely chop the remainder.

- Stir in the ginger, garlic and tamarind paste. Stir in the mango purée, then add the mango chunks.

- Cover and chill in the fridge for 24 hours to allow the flavours to develop.

Thai-style Green Salad

This is also nice with some sweet young pink pickled ginger (*gari*) sprinkled over, if you have some (a vaccum pack of it will keep for ages in a sealed container in the fridge). The natural-coloured pickled ginger tends to be salty, not sweet, so choose carefully.

- Mix the vegetables in a bowl.

- Put the pak choi, coriander, daikon and spring onions in a bowl.

- Whisk the sunflower oil, fish sauce, soy sauce and sugar together until the sugar has dissolved.

- Pour over the salad, toss and serve.

Ingredients:
2 pak choi, finely shredded
Large handful coriander
    leaves, picked off the stalks
¼ daikon (or 1 turnip), grated
2 spring onions, chopped
2 tbsp sunflower oil
2 tsp Thai fish sauce
1 tbsp light soy sauce
½ tsp soft light brown sugar

Serves 4 • Indian

Carrot and Beetroot Salad with Mustard Yoghurt Dressing

Ingredients:
2 large carrots
2 raw beetroot
1 tbsp lemon juice
Salt and freshly ground black
  pepper
2 tbsp sunflower oil
1 tbsp black mustard seeds
4 tbsp thick plain yoghurt
½ tsp clear honey

Carrots and beetroot blend beautifully together. If you have a food processor, use it to grate the vegetables, it saves time and the danger of shredding your fingers too! It's best to wear rubber gloves when preparing beetroot as they stain your hands terribly!

- Peel and grate the carrots and beetroot into a salad bowl. Add the lemon juice and a sprinkling of salt and freshly ground black pepper. Toss gently.

- Heat the oil in a frying pan. Add the mustard seeds and fry for about 30 seconds until they start to pop. Remove from the heat.

- Whisk the yoghurt with the honey until completely blended. Add a pinch of salt. Whisk in the oil and mustard seeds until blended. Pour over the vegetables, toss well and serve.

Preparation time:
10 minutes
Cooking time:
30 seconds
Not suitable for freezing

Mixed Salad with Cumin and Onion Seed Dressing

You can use this dressing with any combination of salad ingredients you like. It makes a great accompaniment to Indian dishes in particular, but try it with other spicy dishes and I'm sure you'll enjoy the fusion of flavours.

- Put all the prepared vegetables except the lettuce leaves and coriander in a bowl.

- Heat the oil in a small frying pan. Add the cumin and black onion seeds and fry for 30 seconds until they become fragrant. Remove from the heat and stir in the remaining dressing ingredients, seasoning to taste with salt and pepper.

- Pour over the salad and toss gently.

- Pile onto gem lettuce leaves in individual serving bowls and scatter the coriander over.

Ingredients:
4 tomatoes, cut in wedges
1 red onion, cut in small wedges and separated in layers
¼ cucumber, peeled and diced
2 celery sticks, peeled and sliced
¼ small daikon peeled and diced (or 12 radishes, halved)

For the dressing
4 tbsp sunflower oil
1 tbsp cumin seeds
1 tbsp black onion seeds
3 tbsp lemon juice
½ tsp Dijon mustard
1 tsp soft light brown sugar
Salt and freshly ground black pepper

To garnish
Gem lettuce leaves
Handful of torn coriander leaves

Preparation time:
10 minutes
Cooking time:
30 seconds
Not suitable for freezing

Serves 4 • Indian

Spiced Green Salad

Ingredients:
1 ripe avocado, stoned,
    peeled and diced
Squeeze of lemon juice
Bag of mixed salad leaves
1 small red onion, sliced
Gem lettuce leaves
Handful of torn coriander
    leaves

For the dressing
4 tbsp sunflower oil
1 tbsp cumin seeds
1 tbsp black onion seeds
3 tbsp lemon juice
½ tsp Dijon mustard
1 tsp soft light brown sugar
Salt and freshly ground black
    pepper

A great little salad to team with almost anything – especially the spicy curries in this collection – you can use whichever style of mixed salad leaves you prefer, sharpened with the onion and made more interesting with the avocado.

- Toss the avocado in the lemon juice, then put in a bowl with the salad leaves and onion.

- Heat the oil in a small frying pan. Add the cumin and black onion seeds and fry for 30 seconds until they become fragrant. Remove from the heat and stir in the remaining dressing ingredients, seasoning to taste with salt and pepper.

- Pour over the salad and toss gently.

- Pile onto gem lettuce leaves in individual serving bowls and scatter the coriander over.

Preparation time:
5 minutes
Cooking time:
1 minutes
Not suitable for freezing

Beansprout and Black Mustard Seed Salad

This is great served with any of the Chinese- or the Japanese-style curries. It's crisp, light and packed with ingredients that complement the Oriental flavours in the main dishes. It's also a very healthy combination of ingredients.

- Mix the prepared vegetables with the beansprouts in a salad bowl.

- Heat the oil in a small frying pan. Add the mustard seeds and fry until they start to pop. Quickly add the soy sauce and rice vinegar, stirring.

- Pour over the salad. Toss and serve whilst still slightly warm.

Ingredients:
¼ cucumber, peeled and diced
1 green or red pepper, deseeded and thinly sliced
2 spring onions, trimmed and cut in diagonal short lengths
100g fresh beansprouts
2 tbsp sunflower oil
2 tbsp black mustard seeds
1 tbsp light soy sauce
1 tbsp rice vinegar

Preparation time:
10 minutes
Not suitable for freezing

Serves 4 • Caribbean

Avocado Sambal

Ingredients:
- 1 just-ripe avocado, peeled, stoned and finely diced
- 1 small red onion, finely chopped
- ½ small mango or papaya, peeled, flesh removed and diced
- 2 tomatoes, skinned, deseeded and chopped
- 1 red pepper, deseeded and chopped
- 5cm piece of cucumber, deseeded and chopped
- Juice of 1 lime
- 2 tsp crushed dried chillies
- 2 tbsp chopped fresh or frozen coriander
- A pinch of coarse sea salt
- Freshly ground black pepper

This goes with curries from all over the globe from the Caribbean to India so call it a salsa or relish if it suits the cuisine better! Make it an hour or so before serving, if time, to allow the flavours to develop but not too long as the avocado loses its texture and may start to discolour.

- Mix together all the ingredients, seasoning to taste with pepper. Spoon the relish into a small dish.
- Chill until ready to serve.

Sweet Chilli Dipping Sauce

Preparation time:
10 minutes
Cooking time:
3 minutes plus standing time
Not suitable for freezing

This is the clear, slightly gooey sauce you buy in bottles – do give it a try. Keep it in the fridge and use within a month. It's very satisfying making your own sauce (and useful if you don't happen to have a bottle of it to hand!).

Ingredients:
280ml water
2 thin red chillies, very finely chopped
2 fat red chillies, very finely chopped
1 tbsp crushed dried chillies
2 large garlic cloves, crushed (or 2 tsp garlic purée)
1 tbsp red wine vinegar
4 tbsp caster sugar
2 tbsp arrowroot

- Set 2 tbsp of water aside in a small bowl. Put the 250ml water in a saucepan with the remaining ingredients except the arrowroot. Cover, bring to the boil, turn off the heat and leave to infuse for at least 30 minutes.

- Blend the arrowroot with the reserved water in the bowl until smooth. Bring the chilli mixture back to the boil, stir in the arrowroot and continue to cook until thickened and clear. Leave to cool slightly.

- Pour into a sterilised screw-topped bottle or jar. Screw on the lid. When cold, store in the fridge.

Serves 4 • Indian

Sweet Mango Lassi

Ingredients:
300ml cold milk
300ml thick plain yogurt
100ml cold water
400ml mango purée (fresh
   or unsweetened, canned)
2 tbsp lime juice
1 tbsp caster sugar

You can use strawberry purée instead of mango or even omit the fruit purée and try it flavoured with a dash of rosewater and lemon or lime (and sweeten it to taste). For extra chill, add a few ice cubes either before or after blending.

• Blend all the ingredients in a blender until frothy.
• Pour into glasses over ice and serve.

• Rice and Other Accompaniments

Mild Salted Lassi with Mint and Cucumber

This is so cooling and refreshing, I love it with a very hot curry or just as a delicious drink on a hot afternoon. You can use melon instead of cucumber for a slightly sweeter version.

- Blend all the ingredients in a blender until smooth and frothy.
- Pour into glasses over ice and serve.

Ingredients:
300ml cold milk
300ml thick plain yogurt
100ml water
½ tsp salt
Good handful fresh mint
    leaves (or 2 tsp dried)
¼ cucumber, peeled and cut
    in chunks

Spiced Desserts

This is a book about curries, celebrating all the wonderful, fragrant sweet and hot spices that influence each one of them from whichever part of the world they originate. I always enjoy something sweet at the end of a meal and I thought it would be a wonderful idea to incorporate some of those heady scents and flavours in some delicious, light desserts to round off any spicy meal. Chillies have long been favourite partners with both chocolate and strawberries but did you know that cloves marry particularly well with white chocolate, or that pears steeped in cinnamon and star anise take on a real depth of flavour? If time is short, serve seasonal fruits threaded on to wooden skewers and brushed with lime-flavoured yoghurt spiked with ground cinnamon. Well, these, plus other delicious combinations will, I hope round off your meals, and this book to perfection.

Chai Ice-cream

Ingredients:
400ml milk
4 chai tea bags
1 vanilla pod
2 eggs
115g caster sugar
1 tbsp cornflour
300ml double cream

To decorate
Ground cinnamon

To serve
Thin chocolate coated
   biscuits

I have only recently got into chai – the lovely spiced Indian tea – and I am addicted to it. It occurred to me that, green tea ice-cream is popular and chai would make a delicious one too! Adding cornflour to the custard stops it curdling so it can be thickened way more quickly than with eggs alone.

- Bring the milk to the boil in a saucepan with the tea bags. Remove from the heat and leave to infuse for at least 10 minutes. Squeeze the bags well to extract maximum flavour, then discard.

- Split the vanilla pod, scrape the seeds into the milk (reserve the pod to use to flavour another dish).

- Whisk the egg, sugar and cornflour together until thick and pale. Gradually whisk the infused milk into the egg mixture.

- Tip back into the saucepan and bring to the boil and simmer for 1 minute until thickened, stirring all the time. Cover with a piece of damp greaseproof paper and set aside to cool.

- Lightly whip the cream and fold into the custard with a metal spoon. Freeze in an ice-cream maker then tip into a freeezerproof container, cover and store in the freezer. Alternatively, tip into a freezerproof container and freeze for about 2 hours until firm around the edges. Whisk with a fork or electric whisk to break up the ice crystals, return to the freezer and freeze until firm.

- Remove from the freezer 10 minutes before serving. Decorate scoops with a dusting of ground cinnamon and serve with thin chocolate biscuits.

Serves 6 • Fusion

Chilli Chocolate Fondants

Preparation time:
20 minutes
Cooking time:
10 minutes
Not suitable for freezing

The pairing of chocolate and chilli has been around since before the Incas, and fondant is not new, but this delicious recipe offers a simple way of combining them. The trick is not to overcook them, so the centre stays gooey when cut open.

- Preheat oven to 220°C/Gas 7. Oil 6 ramekin dishes or dariole moulds set on a baking sheet.

- Melt the butter and chocolate in a bowl over a pan of gently simmering water. Stir well to combine.

- Using an electric whisk, whisk the eggs and sugar until thick and pale and the mixture leaves a trail when lifted out of the mixture. Whisk in the melted chocolate and butter.

- Sift the flour, cocoa and chilli powder over the surface and gently fold in with a metal spoon in a figure of eight movement. Divide the mixture between the prepared ramekin dishes. Bake in the oven for 10 minutes.

- Remove from the oven and leave to cool for a few minutes. Loosen the edges with a round-bladed knife, then turn out onto serving plates.

- Mix the icing sugar, a pinch of chilli powder and cinnamon together and dust over the tops through a small sieve (I use a tea strainer). Serve with whipped or clotted cream.

Ingredients:
100g butter, diced
125g dark chocolate, broken in to pieces
4 eggs
150g caster sugar
85g plain flour
30g cocoa powder
½ tsp chilli powder plus extra for decoration
A little oil for greasing
1 tbsp icing sugar
¼ tsp ground cinnamon

To serve
Whipped or clotted cream

Preparation time:
10 minutes plus chilling
Not suitable for freezing

Serves 4 • Caribbean

Mango Fool

Ingredients:
1 ripe mango
½ fat green chilli, deseeded
    and chopped
2 tbsp lime juice
1 tbsp caster sugar
425g can of custard
300ml double cream
2 gingernut biscuits, crushed

This is quick and delicious and very refreshing to serve after a spicy curry. There's a little kick of chilli and a hint of ginger from the topping. It's also remarkably quick to put together so you can enjoy it any time you fancy an interesting dessert.

- Peel the mango and cut all the flesh off the stone. Place in a blender with the chilli, lime juice and sugar. Blend until smooth.

- Tip into a bowl and fold in the custard.

- Lightly whip the cream until softly peaking and fold half into the fool. Spoon into glasses.

- Whip the remaining cream slightly firmer but still spreadable. Spoon on top of the fools and chill.

- Sprinkle with the crushed gingernuts just before serving.

Caramelised Pineapple and Banana with Buttered Rum

Prepara.
15 m.
Cooking time.
6 minutes
Not suitable for freezing

A taste of the Caribbean here! Make sure your bananas are firm and not too soft or they will go rather pulpy when cooked. If fresh pineapples aren't available, you could use a drained can of pineapple slices in natural juice.

Ingredients:
1 small pineapple
2 firm bananas
5 tbsp soft light brown sugar
1 tsp mixed spice
75g butter
3 tbsp rum
3 tbsp pineapple or orange juice

To serve
Vanilla ice-cream

- Cut off the top and base of the pineapple, then stand it upright and cut down through the rind all round to remove the rind in thick strips. Place the fruit on its side and cut in 4 slices. Cut out the central core. Peel the bananas, cut in halves widthways, then in halves lengthways.

- Place the fruit in a shallow dish. Mix the sugar and spice together and sprinkle over both sides of the fruit to coat completely.

- Melt the butter in a large frying pan. Add the fruit and fry quickly for 2–3 minutes until caramelised underneath. Carefully turn the pieces over and fry until the other sides are browned and caramelised too.

- Carefully lift out of the pan onto serving plates. Add the rum and juice to the pan, bring to the boil, stirring and boil until thickened and syrupy. Spoon over the fruit and serve with vanilla ice-cream.

Serves 6 • British

Chilli Strawberries in Pink Fizz

Ingredients:

350g small strawberries, hulled but left whole

3 fat red chillies, deseeded and finely chopped

Grated zest of 1 orange

6 tbsp caster sugar

4 tbsp orange liqueur

1 bottle sparkling wine such as Prosecco or Rosado, chilled

This is a fabulous way to end a summer party meal – particularly something like the elegant lamb shanks on page 87. You need to use all the chillies to get that little kick as you eat and drink so be bold – it's worth it!

- Put the strawberries in a plastic container with a lid. Add the chillies, orange zest, sugar and liqueur. Toss well. Cover and chill for at least 1 hour but no longer than 3 hours.

- When ready to serve, divide the fruit and juices between 6 champagne flutes. Top up with the sparkling wine and serve with long spoons to eat the fruit, then drink the fizz. Top up with the remaining fizz once some of the fruit is eaten.

Hot Spiced Pears in Cider

Preparat
10 mi
Cooking time
15–20 minutes
Freezeable for:
12 months

Pears are often poached in red wine but the apple flavour of cider enhances their subtle taste beautifully while the sweet spices add a warming fragrance. Try poaching quinces the same way but increase the sugar to 200g.

- Peel the pears, scoop out the cores in the base with a teaspoon or melon baller but leave the stalks intact.

- Put the sugar, cider and spices in a large saucepan. Heat gently, stirring occasionally, until the sugar melts. Lay the pears in the syrup and bring to the boil, reduce the heat, cover and poach gently for about 10 minutes, turning once or twice so they are evenly coloured by the liquid. Once translucent but still holding their shape, carefully lift out with a draining spoon and drain on kitchen paper.

- Boil the syrup rapidly until well reduced and syrupy. Carefully remove the spices.

- Place the pears on small shallow serving bowls and spoon the syrup over. Garnish with tiny sprigs of mint and serve with crème fraîche.

Ingredients:
4 pears
100g caster sugar
300ml dry cider
2 star anise
1 piece of cinnamon stick
1 vanilla pod, split (use one you've already scraped out the seeds from if you have one)

To serve
Mint sprigs
Crème fraîche

Serves 4 • British

White Chocolate and Cinnamon Mousse

Ingredients:
150g white chocolate,
   broken into pieces
2 eggs, separated
150ml double cream
40g caster sugar
½ tsp ground cinnamon

For the coulis
300g fresh or thawed, frozen
   raspberries
4 tbsp icing sugar
Grated zest of 1 lime

To decorate
A little dark chocolate

Cinnamon has a lovely warming scent and blends beautifully with white chocolate to make a soothing, velvety mousse. You must whisk egg whites with clean utensils, so whisking the ingredients in this order means you don't have to wash the beaters in between.

- Melt the chocolate in a bowl over a pan of gently simmering water without stirring, taking care that the bowl does not touch the water.

- Meanwhile, using an electric whisk, whisk the egg whites until stiff and whisk in 1 tsp of the sugar.

- Whip the cream until softly peaking.

- Whisk the egg yolks, remaining sugar and cinnamon until thick and pale.

- Whisk the chocolate into the egg yolks and sugar mixture, then fold in the whipped cream and, lastly, the whisked egg whites. Turn into glasses or ramekin dishes and chill until firm.

- Meanwhile, make the coulis. Purée the fruit in a blender or food processor with the icing sugar and lime zest. Rub through a fine sieve to remove the seeds. Pour into a small jug and chill.

- When ready to serve, grate a little dark chocolate over each mousse and serve with the coulis handed separately.

Cardamom, Honey and Yoghurt Sorbet

Preparation time:
10 minutes plus freezing
Cooking time:
3 minutes, plus freezing

Very fragrant and sweet, yet sharp, this makes a cool and refreshing end to any Indian-style or Asian-style meal. You can cheat and use 4 tbsp bottled lemon juice and omit the decoration if time is short but you will get the best flavour from fresh lemons.

Ingredients:
75g caster sugar
4 tbsp clear honey
300ml water
Thinly pared zest of 2 lemons, cut in thin strips
Juice of 2 lemons
8 cardamom pods, split
500ml creamy, plain yoghurt

- Put the sugar, honey, water, lemon zest and juice, and the cardamom pods in a saucepan. Heat gently, stirring occasionally until the sugar melts. Bring to the boil and boil for 3 minutes. Leave to cool.

- When cold, strain into a separate bowl. Carefully pick out the lemon zest strips and reserve for decoration. Stir the yoghurt into the syrup.

- Either freeze in an ice-cream maker until firm and then tip into a freezerproof container, seal and store in the freezer or tip directly into a freezerproof container, cover and freezer for 2–3 hours until firm around the edges. Whisk with a fork or electric whisk to break up the ice crystals then freeze for a further 2 hours, whisk and freeze again until firm.

- Remove from the freezer 15 minutes before serving. Scoop into glasses and decorate with the lemon zest strips.

Index